Thomas Binney

Money

a popular exposition in rough notes

Thomas Binney

Money
a popular exposition in rough notes

ISBN/EAN: 9783744741453

Printed in Europe, USA, Canada, Australia, Japan

Cover: Foto ©Suzi / pixelio.de

More available books at **www.hansebooks.com**

Money:

A POPULAR EXPOSITION

IN

Rough Notes.

WITH REMARKS ON

STEWARDSHIP AND SYSTEMATIC BENEFICENCE.

BY

T. BINNEY.

"How quickly nature
Falls to revolt, when gold becomes her object."
SHAKSPEARE.
"Put not your trust in money, but put your money in trust." "It is like manure, of very little use except it be spread."
HOLMES. BACON.

FOURTH THOUSAND.

London:
JACKSON, WALFORD, AND HODDER,
27, PATERNOSTER ROW.

TO

SAMUEL MORLEY, Esq.,

IN

TESTIMONY OF A LONG FRIENDSHIP,

AND

AS A SMALL TOKEN OF

RESPECT FOR ONE WHO PRACTICALLY

ILLUSTRATES ITS PRINCIPLES,

THIS BOOK

IS INSCRIBED

BY THE AUTHOR.

PREFACE.

THE following Sermons were delivered in compliance with a request that I would bring before my congregation the claims of the "Systematic Beneficence" Society. I meant to confine myself to *two*, but they grew into fourteen! From the form in which the first appears—"Introductory Section"—it will be seen that my intention was to re-write them, and to put them into the chapters of a Book instead of printing them as a series of sermons. This, however, repeated and severe attacks of illness rendered utterly impossible. It was determined therefore to print the sermons as originally written for the pulpit, and hence the descriptive phrase on the title-page—"a popular exposition *in rough notes.*" The principal exception to this, is in what formed the sixth sermon of the course. This having been delivered without being written, had of necessity to be written afterwards.

It constitutes sermons fifth and sixth of the present volume, with the Concluding Section to Part First.

It can hardly be expected that all that appears here, is exactly what would have been said had my original purpose been carried out. Some statements would, no doubt, have been modified, others omitted: many passages would have been reduced, some enlarged.* From the circumstances, however, already referred to, hardly any thing of this sort has been possible. Still, I am willing to hope that thoughts, *not hastily formed*, though mostly put into words under pressure, may have something in them not altogether worthless: and that the loving God, "who giveth to all liberally," will not withhold his blessing from this sincere though humble endeavour to serve Him.

T. B.

UPPER CLAPTON,
    Nov. 8th, 1864.

---

* While the sheets were passing through the press, two or three additional illustrative texts occurred to me, which had not been noticed when the sermons were written. I could only regret the oversight.

CONTENTS.

Introductory Section.

Truth and Duty.—The ideal.—Departures from it.—Popish abuses.—Protestant shortcomings.—Mammon.—Proposed object of the Book .... 1—15

PART FIRST.

Money may be a Bad Thing.

Money in itself simply a power.—Changes with men's moral relation to it.—The dark side in outline, to be filled up.—*General principle, as announced by Jesus.—Illustrated by Him.—positively, negatively.*—FACTS, SHEWING THE WORKING OF THE MONEY-LUST; first, *in resisting the acceptance of Truth*, and obstructing a man's entrance into the kingdom of God :—The Pharisees.—The Young Ruler.—The man who wished Jesus to speak to his brother.—Elymas.—The masters of the possessed damsel.—Demetrius, the silversmith.—Those to whom the Gospel was hid. *In its antagonism to religious impressions, and to the rise, progress, and perfecting of inward and outward obedience.*—Parable of the Sower.—The Disciples who withdrew.—The Chief Rulers.—The Apostles.—Felix.—Simon Magus.—*In the Church.*—

Ananias and Sapphira.—"They that will be rich."—"Enemies to the Cross."—*Among ministers.*—Teachers of error "for filthy lucre's sake."—Gain and Godliness.—"All seek their own."—Demas.—*The future.*—Predicted developments.—"Grievous wolves."—Bidding for disciples by "perverse things," and "Lies spoken in hypocrisy."—The flock "not spared."—To be "made merchandize of."—Disastrous effects on the people.—*Ultimate issues in a future world.*—The Great Biography.—A peculiar characteristic of Christ's teaching.—The rich proprietor.—In the midst of life, death.—The rich man who "lifted up his eyes in hell, being in torments."—Judas, who went to "his own place."—Gold and silver "eating the flesh as it were fire."—The curtain suddenly dropped .... 17—127

Concluding section to Part First.—Apostolic statements that may be looked at in the light of the preceding argument.—On Covetousness.—On official superiority to the love of money.—On the Apostles' consciousness of clean hands.—On Paul's disinterestedness, prudence, and wisdom.—Peter and John .... 128—142

PART SECOND.

Money may be put to a very good Use.

Preliminary remarks.—What is to be done.—The First proposition.—*Beneficent acts matter of obligation.*—Teaching of Jesus on alms and almsgiving.—The authentic "tradition" of Him.—Apostolic injunctions and implications.—The sphere of the duty unlimited.—A possible objection anticipated and met.—*Second Proposition.*—BENEFICENT ACTS ARE PECULIARLY ACCEPTABLE AND PLEASING TO GOD.—"With such sacrifices God is well pleased."—"An odour of a sweet smell."—"In Him we see the Father."—The penitent woman.—Mary of Bethany.—The widow's mite.—Modifying remarks.—Splendid sins.—Love beautifies all things.—Robbery for burnt-offering.—*Third Proposition.*—BENEFICENT ACTS ARE HELD BY GOD IN SPECIAL REMEMBRANCE.—Cornelius.—Good deeds "a memorial before God."—The Hebrew Christians.—"God is not unrighteous to forget."—*Fourth Proposition.*—BENEFICENT ACTS FOLLOWED BY REWARD.—The Christian doctrine of reward; its certainty and significancy as a general truth.—In respect to beneficence; promised by Christ.—Enjoyed now in two forms, temporal and spiritual.—The primitive deaconess.—Epaphroditus.—Dorcas.—The Centurion.—A general Law.—"Angels unawares."—"All things clean."—"If thou wilt be perfect."—The merciful and the unmerciful.—How the rich are to die easy.—Intercessory prayer.—Treasure laid up in heaven.—Reserved till the resurrection of the just.—Teaching and experience of St. Paul.—The free gift.—The goal and prize.—The joy of the Lord.—"Ye did it unto me."—The abundant entrance and glad welcome into "the everlasting habitations." .... 143—258

PART THIRD.

Stewardship and Systematic Beneficence.

STEWARDSHIP.—All are stewards.—A backward glance, and result of the review.—Secular stewardship.—Service elevated and dignified by confidence.—Spiritual stewardship.—The stewardship of money.—Conscientious spending, saving, and giving.—The analogy between the secular and spiritual in their

	PAGES
characteristics and issues.—The true riches.—The ultimate possession	259—280

SYSTEMATIC BENEFICENCE. — St. Paul recommends "laying by on the first day of the week."—Paley's Exposition.—"The being charitable on a plan."—Paul's rule special and temporary.—Advice, not Law.—"Profitable to direct."—The rule explained.—How to be carried out.—No specified assessment.—Proportionate giving required.—Amount left to the conscience of every man.—The Old Dispensation.—Tithes.—How many?—Enquiry.—Result.—No rule to be drawn from Jewish law to limit or regulate Christian liberty.—Closing appeals.—Some rich men's mistakes.—"Always giving!"—The modern form of "persecution."—A suggestion for changing worry and complaint into thankfulness and joy.—Another to make giving easy.—Not law but love.—I "beseech," though I might "enjoin."—"Thou owest me thine own self."—Devoting a tenth.—Good, but not applicable to all.—The poor clerk.—The rich millionaire.—Beneficent acts required sometimes to be public.—Importance of unconsciousness.—"Hoping for nothing again," not even thanks.—The rich amenable to the judgment of others.—The Weekly Offering............ 281—314

MONEY.

Introductory Section.

God of the world and worldlings,
Great Mammon!—greatest God below the sky.
Spencer.

By doing good with his money, a man as it were stamps the image of God upon it, and makes it pass current for the merchandise of heaven.
Rutledge.

Introductory.

THE Bible, though wonderfully diversified in its contents, resolves itself into a great system of truth and duty. It has doctrinal statements setting forth things to be believed; practical rules inculcating what is to be done. It is sufficient, for our present purpose, to put the matter in this way, although we are quite aware that Believing and Doing by no means include every thing that God requires or that man can render. Between thought and action—true thought and right action—there comes in the vital and vitalizing power of the affections. Light in the reason must become life in the heart, if it is to produce acceptable, visible obedience. "Faith works by love;" —"Love fulfils the law." Love is the daughter of faith, and the mother of virtue. What blood is to the bodily life, love is to that of the spirit. Things to be believed and things to be done represent, respectively, the seed and the fruit. *Between* these two a process intervenes, by which the one is evolved from the other. When we speak with approval of either faith or works, believing or doing, it is with the implied understanding that neither exists alone; that truth believed has become truth felt,—the right thought having sunk into the warm soil of the affections and expanded into life: or, that the right doing commended, is the outgrowth and issue of an inner life as its root or source.

I.

This being understood, we may take up again our first statement, and be allowed to say, that the Scriptures contain "a great system of Truth and Duty." Now this system as it exists in the Bible, is of course complete and perfect. The stars overhead (objective truths) as Divine lights, are all there; *there* in their proper places, orderly arrangement, just relations to one another; each shining with the degree of effulgence properly belonging to it according to its splendour and magnitude. There, too, are the different virtues and graces with which man's life upon earth is to be adorned; and these, also, are set forth in their proper order, relations, and aspects, so that the whole, as thus arranged and delineated, exhibit to us the ideal of a full grown and perfectly developed godlike man. Now, Christian Churches, in their creeds and confessions and types of character—and in their corresponding dogmatic and practical teaching—ought to hold and exhibit all the elements of Truth and Duty, exactly as they lie in the Divine word, in respect to order, relation, proportion, and so on. In like manner, Christian men, individually considered, ought to receive on their reason the accurate impression of all truth, and to exemplify in practice the harmonious development of all virtue. Seeing, however, that this absolute perfection cannot be looked for in either churches or men, we must content ourselves with saying, that it behoves all—communities and individuals alike—to see to it, that, as far as they possibly can, as far as all things necessary to be allowed for permit, they strive after and "press towards" this ideal completeness—the just apprehension of all that the Bible reveals to faith, the full manifestation of all that the Bible demands of love.

Such is the law under which the Church must be supposed to live. We may next notice that there are two ways in which individuals and Bodies may offend against this law, without either of them adopting any positive error, or sinking into gross, practical criminality. In the first place, they may give to some one doctrine or duty, such special and disproportionate attention as may detach it from its proper place and use in the system, and thus make it an entirely different thing from what it really is in the Divine word. Or, secondly, they may so overlook or disregard some particular duty or truth, that, to them, it shall virtually drop out of the system altogether; all that they regard may be true and right, but they do not regard all that is Divinely inculcated as right and true.

Both are wrong. Both offend, though in different ways, against the same law. Now, these two forms of offence are not only to be alike deprecated, but it is to be noted, that they may be fallen into in respect to very important points. If so, they may then operate on Christian thought and life with a malignity like that of positive error. If, without denying the daily motion of the earth on its axis, a person never thought of, or mentioned, or admitted into his calculations any thing but that of its annual progress round the sun;— or, if another, in describing and classifying the productions of *the world*, left out every thing to be found within the tropics;—it is evident that neither of them could have in himself, or could give to others, a just and true notion of the planet we occupy, or the system to which it belongs.

From the nature of the case—the way in which the Bible speaks and is put together, the limitation of the human faculties, the innumerable influences which affect successive generations, particular communities and individual men—it is inevitable that manifold diversities of apprehension and habit, as to Truth and Duty, must be looked for; and, so long as these co-exist with moderation and charity, good may result from them as well as evil. It is to be feared, however, that almost all the sections of the professing Church are open to rebuke for attaching to some one or two points an exaggerated importance, giving them undue prominence, displacing them from their just relations to the other parts of the general system, and thus overlooking and virtually ignoring some depressed and neglected truth. Thus, some continually insist on things to be believed, seldom adverting to what is to be done; or they harp on some particular doctrine or doctrines, to the neglect of the rest: while others again, with uniform iteration, commend and enforce what is "just," and "pure," "good" and "becoming," with little or no reference to the objects of faith. In one community, the great things may be the Priesthood, the Sacraments, the Church; in another, matters of speculation put argumentatively before the understanding. Here you are lulled by the constant murmur of the words of peace and the waters of comfort; there, you are alarmed by a ceaseless call for the bitterness of repentance and the baptism of tears.

Times of religious reaction naturally give rise to exorbitancy and onesidedness of opinion. Reformation comes to be required by some error or abuse which gets to be acknowledged and can no longer be endured. But all errors spring up in the neighbourhood of some truth; they grow round about it, and, for the most part, derive their strength from such contiguity. When, then, the mind of a church or of a nation is aroused, and the axe of reform is brought forth and laid at the root of the tree,—when the heart is pulsating with a fervid zeal, and the hand and arm strong and steady from resolute purpose,—there is great danger of error and truth being cut down and rooted out together. The human mind is prone to extremes; especially so, in popular action. Indeed, the most of reformers are not only men of one idea, but they generally speak and act as if they were quite certain that the extreme opposite to wrong must be right. Their tendency, therefore, is to advocate and aim at that extreme. Different ages have done, and different parties in the Church do this. One after another Communities have arisen exaggerating one or two points, and almost losing sight of every thing else. They have thus cut, so to speak, the great system of Truth into pieces; each has seized on a separate portion, and, exulting in the possession of it, keeps holding it up as if it were the whole. A *living* body does not consist of so many separate limbs and members. There must be organic completeness, if there is to be vital action. There may be life, indeed, and strength too, where a limb has been lost, or an arm wounded. So, Churches, Systems, and individual Christian men must, we suppose, be charitably regarded as holding (and being) what is alive, though maimed,—rather than as each treasuring (or constituting) a withered or dead hand or foot.

II.

These remarks bear upon, and may serve to introduce, the subject about to be discussed in this book, namely, the Christian doctrine of pecuniary beneficence :—*the stewardship of money*, and of all that money signifies or can be made to represent.

The devotement of wealth to the honour of God, to the use of the Church, and in provision for the poor, was carried to such extreme length in Popish times, that numbers, as it has been said, "found themselves beggars because their fathers had been saints." There could not but come a revolt from, and a reaction against such a system; a reaction too, against the doctrinal perversion which exaggerated the worth and merit of good works, (especially in the form of money-giving) to so enormous an extent as to shock the reason. The extravagance and impiety of what was taught on this subject at a particular time, was one of the sparks which, falling on the fuel that had been secretly accumulating in men's souls, was followed by a conflagration that revealed to the popular eye the corruptions of the Papacy. Money was wanted to carry on and complete the magnificent structure which was rising in Rome to the honour of St. Peter. To give it, was not only represented as a thing beautiful and becoming in the children of the Church, but the virtue and value of the act—its power to procure for the giver immunity from the consequences of crime —were set forth with such coarse illustrations, such outrageous extravagance, not to say blasphemy, that men were provoked to contradiction and resistance, and an explosion followed, the effects of which continue to this day. Then began the tearing away from the temple of truth, of the weeds and parasites and suckers of superstition, the growth and accumulation of centuries, which had covered the building, had concealed its beauty and injured its strength. The revival of apostolical preaching in the announcement of the doctrine of justification by faith, struck at the root of all that had been taught, or that ignorance had been suffered to believe, of the possibility of propitiating God by the offerings and almsdeeds of selfishness and terror. It exposed the delusion that building a church, endowing a monastery, enriching the priesthood, giving to the poor, were efficient forms in which property might be so used as to secure the acceptance of the sinner trembling under the consciousness of crime, and to deliver the penitent from the flames of purgatory—to lessen their intenseness, or to limit their duration.

A reaction against such an extravagant estimate as this of the value of good works, was of course very likely to lead to the denial of their having, in any sense whatever, anything like value or worth at all. In a revolt against what the Scriptures do *not* teach on any given point, the chances are—especially if the abuse be great and the revolt violent—that what they *do* teach will be overlooked, very possibly denied or rejected. Luther, in his zeal for the recovered doctrine of justification by faith, was led to set aside the epistle of St. James, and to denounce it as worthless—a mere handful of chaff—because it seemed to contradict his favourite opinion. He forgot that the same truth may have two sides; and that he who looks only at one of them, instead of having, as he supposes, the thing itself pure and simple, has got, in fact, only the half of it. Faith has something else to do besides being the instrument of justification; and works have other uses besides being the proof or evidence of faith. The error of Popery in relation to the meritoriousness of giving money to God and the poor—error though it was—was founded on certain Divine sayings scattered throughout the Bible; sayings which it perverted, exaggerated, or mistook. It was perfectly natural, that in the recoil of the mind from the error and the comment, the truth and the text might get into danger, and God's own utterances be silenced, ignored, or explained away. It is not to be denied that there are a good many passages of Scripture, inculcating and praising beneficent deeds, of which Protestant preachers are very shy. I purpose to collect, and to set forth in some sort of order, in this book, all that the New Testament says about MONEY;—about the possession of it—in respect to kindness, consideration, and thorough conscientiousness in the ordinary or religious use of it,—with anything else that belongs to its "stewardship," and to all that *that* implies;—and to the results, immediate and ultimate, of fidelity or neglect, and so on. It is quite possible that what the Bible teaches, while it may be much less than what Papists pretend, may yet turn out to be a great deal more than what many Protestants either believe or like.

III.

There is a remarkable expression in the parable of the unjust steward,* which would seem to intimate that Money may be contemplated under two opposite aspects. *It may be a bad thing; but it may be put to a very good use.* Such would seem to be the import of the Divine saying,—"*Make to yourselves friends of the mammon of unrighteousness, that when ye fail they may receive you into everlasting habitations.*" Without, at present, attempting to expound the whole story of the parable in question, it will be sufficient to notice the mixed impression which these words make upon us. Mammon signifies wealth,

* Luke xvi. 9.

riches, worldly property. When it is said, ver. 13, "No servant can serve two masters; .. ye cannot serve God and mammon;" Mammon is personified. It is represented as an idol, which men may be subject to and serve as a god. The words "unrighteous" and "unrighteousness" employed in relation to it, do not mean that riches are always the product of fraud and injustice; but that, if they are "served," looked up to, made an idol of, they will be found to be false and deceitful; that is, they will prove to be "unrighteous" in the sense of promising what they never perform. They will be like a painted bubble which vanishes when grasped; or like "a broken reed" that pierces the hand of him that leans upon it. Like certain teachers who "promised liberty" to their disciples, but who, when believed, left them like themselves in "bondage to corruption," so Riches offer everything, but, being trusted to, are found "to make themselves wings and fly away!" They have not only no quality entitling them to supreme and exclusive confidence, but they are distinguished by other qualities, which (speaking in a figure), lead them knowingly and deliberately to deceive. Mammon *over us*—made the object of affection and faith—will be found in time to have none of the attributes corresponding to such sentiments. The idolator of wealth, like other idolators, will discover one day, that the thing he worships will turn out "a devil and not a god." On the other hand, if, instead of serving mammon, a man compels it to serve *him;* if, instead of making it his master, he uses it as his slave; if, instead of looking up to it, he places it beneath him, makes it look up towards himself, to know his will and do his bidding; if he thus regards it as an instrument, and employs it, as it may be employed, for the promotion of great and good objects :—why then, its very nature will change; it will be faithful and devoted, pure and upright, tender and true, for it will partake the character and be filled with the spirit of its Master and Lord. The great brazen idol—when deposed from its unrighteous pre-eminence, broken to fragments and stamped to dust under the foot of the man who stands over it—will be found to have become most precious. Its dust then turns into living seed, which can be scattered abroad by the strong hand, and sown beside all waters : and which will spring up and be abundantly productive,—productive of that golden grain which is worthy of being gathered into the garner of God. These remarks are sufficient to indicate the meaning of the statement, that we may "*make friends of*"—that is, secure advantages by or through the wise use of—"the unrighteous"—or deceitful and slippery—"mammon." The two ideas which come out of this, may, as we have said, be thus stated :—" Money may be a bad thing;" but, "It may be put to a very good use." It is our purpose to present to the eye of the reader *everything* to be found in the New Testament, that can be employed to illustrate the one or the other of these two statements.

MAMMON led them on:
Mammon, the least erected spirit that fell
From heaven: for e'en in heaven his looks and thoughts
Were always downward bent, admiring more
The riches of heaven's pavement, trodden gold,
Than aught, divine or holy, else enjoyed
In vision beatific: by him first
Men also, and by his suggestion taught,
Ransacked the centre, and with impious hands
Rifled the bowels of their mother earth
For treasure, better hid.
MILTON.

MAMMON has enriched his thousands, and has damned his ten thousands.
SOUTH.

PART FIRST.

Money may be a Bad Thing.

LORD! with what care hast Thou begirt us round;
Parents first season us. Then Schoolmasters
Deliver us to laws. They send us bound
To rules of reason. Holy messengers;
Pulpits and Sundays : sorrow dogging sin;
Afflictions sorted; anguish of all sizes;
Fine nets and stratagems to catch us in!
Bibles laid open; millions of surprises;
Blessings beforehand; ties of gratefulness;
The sounds of glory ringing in our ears;
Without our shame; within our consciences;
Angels and grace; eternal hopes and fears!
Yet all these fences, and their whole array,
One cunning BOSOM SIN *blows quite away.*
GEO. HERBERT.

Sermon I.

Luke xvi. 9.

Make to yourselves friends of the mammon of unrighteousness; that when ye fail they may receive you into everlasting habitations."

IN a previous reference to this passage, we so explained it as to get out of it these two thoughts:—*Money may be a bad thing, but it may be put to a very good use.* Now, that which may be either good or bad, according to circumstances, may in itself be regarded as neither the one nor the other. It is simply a power. But that, it may be urged, is something—something great, if not good. Be it so; still, as such, it is of worth or value only as so much latent capability, so much raw material, which may be turned to different and even opposite purposes. Standing alone, simply looked at as a thing, Money is a neutral, slumbering force. According as it is approached from one side or the other, or as it moves and acts in this direction or that, it becomes revealed as diabolical or divine. Money, as money, is power in repose. Set in motion, it may fall like dew or rush like a whirlwind; it may be light to irradiate, or lightning to destroy. We have nothing to say, then, against money in the abstract. Of course, circumstanced as we are in the life that now is, money is to each of us an absolute necessity. We *must* have some of it, or something of what it represents. So far, therefore, it might be said to be good—good in itself—because it is a good thing to have it, or so much of it as our necessities require. The Scriptures themselves do not condemn riches in the abstract. It is not said that "*money* is the root of all evil"—but "*the love* of it." True, riches may be a temptation, like anything else that is a power for good or evil; but they may also be an aid to virtue,—they may stimulate to fidelity by deepening the sense of moral obligation.

What we have described then, as a neutral slumbering force, is a thing which, so regarded, we are not going to stigmatize and depreciate. We are not here to despise it, or to set it at nought, or to call it bad names. It is useful or pernicious, a blasting or benignant power, *according to the moral relation of an individual to it.* This is the point we have to mark and insist upon. The influence and operation of money on a man, will be according to the man's state of mind; according to the condition of his heart and affections, his estimate and plan of life. Where these are low and worldly, or are suffered to become so; where the nature is inherently gross, sensual, sordid,—or where it is weak, sensitive, impressible, and alive to questionable influences; or where the man ceases to watch and pray; to keep up the tone and attend to the culture of his inner life—in these and all similar cases, *money* may act like a canker and a curse.

This is the aspect of the subject we have to do with to-day. Our business is with the dark side of the thing as it affects the spiritual interests of humanity. We propose showing you—confining ourselves to the New Testament—how, in consequence of the state of the heart, and the wrong relation in which a man may stand towards money, its influence on his religious life may be most disastrous. You will see, as we go on, how wealth faces religion as an antagonist; fights with it, and seeks to thwart and destroy it, at every step, from beginning to end. Money may obstruct the entrance of religion into the soul; it may attack it when it enters; it may resist its continuance there, and rebel against its rule; it may undermine its power; it may seduce its supporters, and corrupt its administration, and produce a variety of the most lamentable results; and, finally, it may sink the soul of its victim into black and bottomless perdition;—when, from being merely as so much "thick clay" with which its toiling and hard-worked slaves lade themselves, it will change into pitch and bitumen,—

and will burst into flame, and "eat their flesh as it were fire!" These general statements we are to support and substantiate, by collecting and classifying some of those pregnant and suggestive utterances which are to be met with among "the true sayings of God."

I.

We begin by noticing the principle which our Lord laid down and largely illustrated at the commencement of his ministry;—the principle, that, if the heart is not cleared of the love of the world, and of the things of the world, there will be no room in it for the love of the Father; or, which comes to the same thing, if the love of God, and of God's service, has not, in any given case, such strength as to repress and expel every base affection, the man cannot be the subject of spiritual life. No man can serve two masters,—two masters whose characters and commands are opposite and contrary the one to the other. Two such masters cannot be served in the sense in which service signifies absolute and entire devotion of heart and soul, brain and hand, to the work which either requires. Such service is like that which is rendered to an object of worship;— service demanded by law, animated by love,—law, regal and authoritative,—love, single and supreme. No man can thus serve two masters. No heart has room in it for two contradictory absorbing sentiments of duty and affection. Ye cannot worship both Baal and Jehovah; "Ye cannot serve God and Mammon."

Often in the course of his ministry our Lord asserted this principle,—a principle indicative at once of the regal character of the religious life, and of what is required as a necessary preliminary preparation for it. But in the sermon on the Mount, He dwells upon the thought;—setting it in different lights, and enforcing it by various illustrations.* For the sake of practical impression, the *substance* of his sayings may be set forth in this way:—'high service, absolute devotion to an object, is like religion;—the central power of which is faith or trust, the principal expression love. If you put your trust in riches, if money or Mammon be your master, "the God of your idolatry," you will expect everything from *it;* you will give it your heart; you will make "gold your hope, and fine gold your confidence." Your supreme desire will be to accumulate it; you will live for that; it will fill your thoughts and form your dreams; it will give colour and shape to all your feelings, and direction and strength to every purpose: and, if so, and so long as it is so, your soul cannot repose with faith on God, nor your heart swell and beat with love to him. Nay, you will be incapable of seeing his glory, of appreciating or discovering his character. Your inward eye, fixed on

* Math. vi. 19—24, 33.

and fastened to another object,—and that object antagonistic to *Him*,—you will be blind to everything else; the understanding will be dark and the conscience dead. The figure of Mammon, the God of this world, standing between you and heaven, will cast its dark shadow upon you, which will be as the darkness of the shadow of death! Therefore I say unto you, "lay not up for yourselves treasures upon earth"—live not for the world, and the things of the world; "but lay up for yourselves treasure in heaven"—live and labour for eternal life,—for, "where your treasure is, there will your heart be also." "The light of the body is the eye; if thine eye be single"—healthy and clear—"thy whole body shall be full of light;" if there is no predominant sordid affection, no grovelling worldliness of aim, disturbing the mental vision and obscuring the moral judgment, thou wilt see all things clearly;—spiritual objects in spiritual light, and "thy whole body shall be full of light;" thy entire spiritual nature shall be at once illuminated and quickened by it. "But if thine eye be evil,"—diseased and sightless as to divine things, from the paralyzing influence of the worship of Mammon, the passion for laying up treasures upon earth, "thy whole body shall be full of darkness;"—for, the very faculty of vision, the moral power to perceive and appreciate spiritual truth being depraved, that which should be light within you being darkness, "how great" and awful will be "that darkness!" "Seek" then "*first*"—with a supreme, predominant, and directing love—"the kingdom of God and His righteousness, and other (the lesser) things shall be added unto you." But, if you seek first,—determine and resolve, at all hazards, to make sure of these lesser things,—the kingdom of God and the righteousness thereof may come nigh unto you;—" they may stand and knock" and ask for admission at the door of your heart; but that heart, filled with the world, will have no room to receive them; nor would they enter and dwell there, unless the world and the love of it were cast out!

Such was the principle laid down by our Lord. This principle he illustrated, not only in its positive but on its negative side.* That is to say, he applied it, not only in relation to the actual laying up of treasure,—successful accumulation; but to the absence of this—the pressure or the fear of want; the absorbing anxiety and mental preoccupation of those, who, in such circumstances, "walk by sight, and not by faith." The man whose trust is in money,—whose exclusive 'confidence is in what he can touch and look at, and feel that he possesses,—if he is destitute of that which constitutes his security—his sole security—against the calls of life, the realities of to-

* Math. vi. 25—32.

day and the possibilities of to-morrow;—why, he will be just as incapable of receiving the kingdom of God, as the man who can "fare sumptuously every day," and "has much good laid up for many years." The world and mammon can as thoroughly fill the heart, in the shape of troubled thought, and fearful forecastings, and anxious care, as in that of complacency and satisfaction from realized possession and "fulness of bread." In neither the one case nor the other, is there fitting space, or light, or air, for the admission and growth of the seed of the kingdom. God may be as much denied and Mammon worshipped, and an antagonism to the truth set up, by absorbing solicitude about prospective and possible want, as by the secular satisfaction produced by a man's having in his hand "all that the heart can wish." He who "loves the world," and who is manifested as such,—either by the pride of success in "laying up treasure," or by the canker of disappointment eating into his soul,—"the love of the Father is not in him." It is not only not in him, but while either mental condition lasts, it cannot be;—by the very constitution of things, by all the laws which govern the mind and regulate thought, it must of necessity be excluded.

II.

Let us now look at some of the New Testament illustrations of the truth of this principle, as seen in the case of particular individuals. We can see a thought more distinctly, and feel it more forcibly, when it is embodied in a fact than when it is only set forth in words. Recall to your mind the following incidents. There were some who not only were unpersuaded or unimpressed by the teaching of Jesus, especially by such of his statements as those just referred to, but who openly "derided" both Him and them. Who were these? "The Pharisees, *who were covetous.*"* They could not receive his sayings; they could not see their truth, or admit their propriety, or feel their force; to *them* they were not only not true, and therefore to be rejected or reasoned against; but they were absurd and ridiculous, and only fit therefore to be spurned and laughed at. The light of the kingdom could not pierce the darkness in which their minds dwelt. Their inward eye was incapable of admitting it. The secret of this is given in the three words into which the description of their character is compressed,—" the Pharisees, who were covetous." *Who were covetous;* —that stroke of the pencil explains all.

But covetousness may signify, not merely the love of money, but any irregularity or exorbitancy of affection in relation to present things; just as the love of the world may be betrayed by either the one or the other of its elements—" the lust of the flesh,

* Luke xvi. 14.

or the lust of the eye, or the pride of life." Now the Pharisees were covetous of the world's applause; they loved to be honoured and distinguished; they did things with a view "to be seen of men," and they sought "the uppermost seats in the synagogue, and the principal places at feasts;" and in consequence of this—this entire and absolute abandonment of themselves to the service of Mammon in this particular form of his worship—our Lord said to them, ' "*How* can ye believe, who receive honour one of another and seek not the honour that cometh from God only?"—The thing is impossible. You are not in a state of mind to understand what I say; to see the beauty or to feel the power of spiritual and divine thought. Of course to *you*,—with your preoccupation of faculty and feeling, your low ambition, your selfish and worldly ends,—of course to you I speak parables, mysteries, utter incredibilities. You *cannot* believe what I teach. The God of this world has blinded your eyes so that the true light cannot shine into you, to enable you to discern the objects which that light reveals to faith. To you, and to all in your mental and moral condition, the words of divine wisdom must sound like madness and folly. They can only be understood by the inner sense seen by the inner eye. But in you that eye is sightless. Mammon and the world are lying so close to it, that they hide all things else, and spread a veil alike on the heart within you and the heaven without. The natural or animal man, the man who has only the senses and the soul quickened, the powers which belong to his lower and material nature—appetite impelled by the desire of the flesh, vanity and ambition by the lust of the eye and the pride of life—" the natural man," whose earthly susceptibilities, the influences of the world (gross, or refined, it matters not) have developed and ripened, but whose higher faculties are as good as dead,—he "*cannot* receive the things of the spirit of God, neither can he know them, because they are spiritually discerned." " I know you, that ye have not the love of God in you." You love not God, because your hearts are full of the love of the world. Loving the world, and the praise of the world, ye cannot believe my words. "*I* receive not honour from men,"—*you* do. I live a life to you inconceivable; I speak a language which *must* sound to you as an unknown tongue; for, as you cannot serve God and Mammon, so, neither can ye understand or believe what I say so long as " ye receive honour one of another, and seek not the honour that cometh from God only." ' *

In this way were the utterances of Our Lord illustrated by facts. In these two instances, we see the influence of Mammon, in the form of the love of money, and the love of distinction, so operating as

* John v. 44.

to obstruct the approach of the truth to the heart and the understanding, and to render the very beginning of the religious life a moral impossibility. The Pharisees—who, indeed, had a religion, such as it was; a religion of form and ceremony and punctilious externalism,—which left them "like whited sepulchres, fair to the eye, but within full of dead men's bones and of all uncleanness,"—the Pharisees, who were covetous, "devouring widows' houses," "making long prayers that they might be seen of men,"—contriving to be at the corner of the streets at the hour of devotion, blowing a trumpet when they dispensed alms, and loving to be bowed to, and robed, and Rabbied;— why, such men were so walled in and enclosed by the flesh, that the kingdom of God, though it came ever so near, *could not touch them.*

We have a different illustration in another case, in which the result is equally disastrous, though the character of the man is more respectable. A young man, earnest and ingenuous apparently, came to Jesus and inquired " what good thing he could do that he might secure and inherit eternal life ? " * It seemed as if he were ready to do any thing. It is probable also, that there was a secret feeling in him, that he was already in possession of all required and commanded virtue, and that what he would have to do, to make things perfectly sure, was some work of

* Math. xix. 19—26.

supererogation,—something above and beyond necessary righteousness. Our Lord took him on this ground, and first gave him, by implication, both instruction and reproof, telling him " to keep the commandments," which, to do perfectly, he would find to be labour sufficient. As our Lord only mentioned those of what we call the second table relating to practical duties—" honour thy father and thy mother, do not steal, do not kill, do not commit adultery"—the young man answered, and might answer truthfully, "all these have I kept from my youth up; *What lack I yet?*" There *was* something lacking,—something which belonged to the very ground and basis of religious virtue,— something necessary to the existence, and constituting the essence and principle of spiritual life. This was the love of God,—the first and great commandment; the love of God, " with all the heart, and with all the soul, and with all the strength,"—love supreme, regal, absolute, which was equal to any requirement, any service, or any sacrifice. Had our Lord replied to the man's second question, by telling him, *even in the terms of the law,* to love God, he might have given the same reply as before,—that he did that, and always had done it; and no one that heard him (but Jesus himself) could have contradicted him. Our Lord, however, instead of merely mentioning the prescribed feeling, applied a practical test. Feeling and sentiment may be professed in words, though they can only be proved and manifested by acts. Hence came forth the word of trial, which was to be as a fire applied to the man to discover whether he was gold, or dross. ' " If thou would'st be perfect,"—if thou would'st visibly evince that, from absolute love to God, thou dost so entirely submit thyself to Him, as to be ready for anything,—if thy heart beats with this supreme affection, which at once prompts and beautifies all true obedience,—I, whom thou approachest and acknowledgest as a prophet,—I, speaking in the divine name, say unto thee as from God, " sell all that thou hast, and give to the poor, and come, take up thy cross, and follow me.'" Touched by this pointed and winged word, the profession and pretensions of the man collapsed in a moment. On hearing what Jesus said he was " very sorry;"—he went away silent and sad, for " he had great possessions ; " " he was very rich."

Now we quite admit, that the test here applied was very severe. But the man invited it; he brought it upon himself; it was the only way, or at least the shortest way, by which he could be taught the lesson that he needed; be made to understand the baselessness of mere external virtue, and the claim of God on the whole heart. "Alas," said Jesus, looking after him more in sorrow than in anger,—for his character was amiable, his wish sincere tho' his will was weak,

—"Alas! how hardly shall they that have riches enter into the kingdom of God. It is easier for a camel to go through the eye of a needle, than for a rich man to enter into the kingdom of God." The disciples were astonished at his words. But he said unto them, ' " children, how hard is it for them that *trust* in riches to enter into the kingdom of God." It is indeed impossible. God is the only proper object of trust: ye cannot be saved but by faith in Him: and you cannot have that while you put your trust and your faith in *them*. The two principles cannot co-exist in the same soul. And they that have riches, are so liable *to trust in them*,—to feel as if they were safe from the fear of evil,—that it is very hard for them "to enter the kingdom." Still, it is possible through the help of God, for " with God all things are possible." He can make a rich man willing to enter the kingdom, leaving his riches at the door. But without God's grace,—and extraordinary grace, —where wealth is in the hand as a possession, Mammon will be in the heart as a power ; and " ye cannot serve God and Mammon." '

III.

Thus are we taught by these several instances, how mighty and malignant is the money-lust, in opposing the entrance of religious light, the coming in of the kingdom of God into a man's soul; or (as put in the other form), how it impedes a man's *approach* to it,— obstructs his going towards it, and getting into it. It sends him back to his miserable confidences, tied and bound to the ear of his idol! The last instance to which we have referred, is very suggestive and very admonitory. All appearances, to the human eye, were pleasing and promising. There was everything to prepossess us in the young man's favour. We might be excused for thinking that he was " not far from the kingdom of God." Nor was he far from it, in one sense,—for the kingdom of God "had come nigh unto him," but however near it might be, it turned out that he would not enter it. He would not enter it, because he was not equal to the personal sacrifice, which, in his case, Jesus required as the test of his sincerity. He turned away from the gate of the kingdom, just as it was being opened to receive him, because it was not large enough to admit both him and his wealth. He seemed earnest, determined, resolute, zealous; but beneath and underlying all appearances, there was one bosom sin,—he loved his money, clung tenaciously to "his large possessions," —kept hold of them as with both hands,—and he had not another with which to take hold of heaven too. So *that* slipped away from him, and he from it. One bosom sin, determinately retained, will harden the heart, stupify the conscience, darken the mind and damn the man! It will resist and overcome inward monitions; it will frustrate and render nugatory all influences from without. " Herod feared John because he was a good and a holy man." He heard him and was touched; " he heard him often and heard him gladly," and "did many things" in consequence; but *there was one thing he would not do;*— he would not put away Herodias. And she,—his bosom sin personified and embodied,—led him at last to send an executioner to behead John in prison! And so here. The young man has done much, and seems ready to do more;—ready to do anything. He stands listening to Christ, looking up to him with a pleased, ingenuous expression, as if prepared to welcome whatever he might say. He could not do it. There was a bosom sin, which lay at the root of his seeming excellence, and which made it wither and fall far sooner than Jonah's gourd.

"For mark the change; thus spake the Lord,
 'Come, part with earth for heaven to-day,'
The youth, astonished at the word,
 In silent sadness went his way."

Sermon II.

Luke xii. 15.

"Take heed, and beware of covetousness; for a man's life consisteth not in the abundance of the things which he possesseth."

WE proceed with our enumeration of Scriptural facts, illustrative of the bad influence of Money when permitted to become Mammon. This influence is to be seen, in the first place, in its obstructing the entrance of light and truth into the soul,—its preventing a man's advance to the kingdom of God, or the approach of the kingdom of God to him. Instances to this effect were adduced last Sunday; others are to be added now.

One day, when our Lord was addressing his disciples in the audience of the multitude, he was led to expatiate on some of the most searching and solemn topics that he could possibly touch.* He dwelt on aspects of truth, which were calculated to lift the soul

* Luke xii. 1—21.

out of the region of low mundane influences, and to reveal to it at once the greatness of humanity, spiritually contemplated, and the grand, calm sublimity of a childlike religious faith. He exposed the meanness and peril of hypocrisy; the certainty of an approaching crisis, when the secret and the real in every man would be revealed, whether it were good or bad. He exhorted his hearers to become superior to apprehension for the body, and to cultivate, rather, reverence for and fear of Him "who could not only kill the body, but after that had power to cast into Hell." He referred to the apparently trivial fact of "five sparrows being sold for a farthing;" but, adding the assurance that "not one of them was forgotten before God," he showed the superiority of man to all inferior natures by the simple statement,—"ye are of more value than many sparrows." He wove into his sayings sublime utterances as to the reality and minuteness of God's providential care, "even the very hairs of your head are all numbered;" and, proceeding to inculcate the duty and necessity of loyalty to Truth at all hazards,—adhesion to the "Son of Man," and steadfastness in confessing Him, whatever the sacrifice,—he concluded with the assurance of future supernatural aid, that would be ready to be imparted at any moment, and would be appropriate and adequate to every emergency.—Amid peril and persecution, in assembly or synagogue, before magistrates and powers, none of His followers need fear that they would be left to become abashed or embarrassed. The weak should be as David, the timid calm, the dumb eloquent;—for they would be filled with the varied gifts of that Divine Spirit, from whom come energy, confidence, magnanimity, elevation, the fitting thought and the burning word. "Take no thought how or what ye shall answer, or what ye shall say; for the Holy Ghost shall teach you in the same hour what ye shall say."

Such discourse, proceeding from one who spake "as never man spake," and whose wonderful thoughts and words so often awed or exalted those who heard him,—such discourse, it might have been expected, would have thrown a sort of divine charm over his audience, which would have repressed or expelled all ideas but those that were in harmony with itself. If ever there was a moment, when, as by a spell, the grossest nature, for the time, might have been elevated, the most sordid refined, the earthliest etherialized, this, surely, was such a moment. And yet, just when a brief pause occasioned a silence— one which ought to have been felt as far too sacred to be rudely broken—some one in the crowd, whose ear and heart were so closed and darkened that he had not understood, or had not felt, the Divine force of the Lord's sayings, cried out—"*Master, speak to my brother that he divide the inheritance with me!*"

The words, if we might so express it, caused a visible shock to the mind of Jesus himself! As he once marvelled at finding such great faith—such unanticipated maturity of trust—in one "not of the house of Israel;" so now he appears to have been surprised by the sudden revelation of such inveterate worldliness of heart, in one who had just been standing beneath the shadow, or rather in the light, of some of the most penetrating and transforming aspects of spiritual truth. For once he betrayed something like disgust as well as indignation, and flung from him the petition and the petitioner with a flash of contempt— "*Man*, who made me a judge or a ruler over you?" Then, turning to those about him, and holding up as it were before them the diseased and shrivelled heart of a worshipper of Mammon, he pointed to it and said, "Take heed, *and beware of covetousness;* for a man's life consisteth not in the abundance of the things which he possesseth." "And he spake a parable unto them, saying, the ground of a certain rich man brought forth plentifully: and he thought within himself, saying, What shall I do, because I have no room where to bestow my fruits? And he said, this will I do: I will pull down my barns, and build greater; and there will I bestow all my fruits and my goods. And I will say to my soul, Soul, thou hast much goods laid up for many years; take thine ease, eat, drink, and be merry. But God said unto him, *thou* fool, this night thy soul shall be required of thee: then whose shall those things be which thou hast provided?"—Here, I can imagine, turning to the man whose unconscious revelation of himself had suggested and called forth the parable, and with his eye resting on him, he said—"*So is he that layeth up treasure for himself and is not rich toward God.*"

In further illustration of the malignant influence of the love of money in corrupting and hardening the heart, and resisting the entrance of truth into the soul, we will take three facts from the Apostolic history,— one out of each of the three great missionary journeys of St. Paul.

I.

The scene of the first is at Paphos, in the island of Cyprus, at the very commencement of the Apostle's travels.* There, in immediate contact with, and seeking to acquire a bad influence over the mind of the Deputy, Sergius Paulus—described by Luke as a "prudent man," known from other sources to have been intelligent and upright—the Apostle found a certain sorcerer, a false prophet, a Jew whose name was Bar-Jesus. This fellow was one of a class of unprincipled men, who at this time went about the

* Acts xiii. 6—11.

world, using the better knowledge which they had as Jews, for bad and selfish purposes :—to make money and get a name by clever tricks and high discourse. He was degenerate Judaism personified; and Paul was Judaism itself, exalted and spiritualized. The one virtually said to the Gentiles, " we seek not you, but *yours*,"—or you only to get yours. The other could declare, with a distinctness and sincerity which could not be gainsayed, " We seek not yours, but *you;*"— you, that you may become " fellow-citizens with the saints and of the household of God." So, the old and the new met. Transcendent advantages, arising from divinely communicated knowledge :—in the one case perverted to base ends and sordid purposes; in the other, sublimated by the highest form of philanthropy, animated by the spirit of self sacrifice.—They came into contact,—confronted each other,—the intelligence and mental activity of the age, in the person of the Proconsul, looking on. Bar-Jesus, or Elymas the Sorcerer, as he is also designated, saw that his honours and emoluments were in danger ; distinction would be forfeited and gain gone, if the Truth, as brought by the Apostles, were accepted. *He* cared nothing for truth ; nor was his mind capable of admitting or appreciating the new aspect and lofty attitude, which the Christian discoveries imparted to the old Hebrew creed.

When the Deputy determined to examine for himself into the message said to be brought by the strangers recently arrived, and therefore "sent for Barnabas and Saul, and desired to hear the Word of God, Elymas withstood them."—He questioned, controverted, blasphemed, "Seeking to turn away the Deputy from the faith." He would neither "go into the kingdom of heaven himself," nor (if he could help it) "would he suffer them that would enter it to go in." The lust of base gain—the desire and pursuit of filthy lucre—lay at the bottom of his character, and made him what he was. It was this which blinded his eye to the true light; closed his heart against the word of salvation; filled his mouth with sophistical objections; and strengthened his purpose, at once to resist Apostolic truth, and to keep his distinguished auditor, or disciple, the slave of delusions and the victim of lies. It was this which found its full and appropriate development in what he had become, as described by Paul, when he held up the mirror to his face to shew him the likeness of himself.—" O, full of all subtlety, and all mischief, thou child of the Devil, thou enemy of all righteousness, wilt thou not cease to pervert the true ways of the Lord?" Then there fell upon the man the most appropriate and significant punishment. "He became blind, and unable for a season to see the sun." The outward and visible sign, this, of that mental and spiritual darkness, which his sin and sordidness had induced;—a darkness which even the beams of the "Sun of righteousness" could not pierce.

II.

The scene of the next fact, an incident belonging to Paul's second apostolic journey, is Philippi.* As at the commencement of the first journey, he had to meet an obstacle to the Gospel in the cupidity of a Jew; in the second, a more emphatically Gentile mission, he had to witness the same thing in the opposition of Gentiles. It was at the commencement, too, of a new era in his life and labours. When he left Antioch "to visit the brethren in every city" where he and Barnabas had previously preached, he had no thought of going beyond the limits of Asia, to which their ministrations had been confined. But he was divinely directed to undertake something far beyond the intention of his will. The time had now come, when he was to leave, for a season, the centre and the neighbourhood of successive revelation, and to carry to the West, to the seats and cities of European intelligence, the momentous message with which he was entrusted. Sailing from Troas and proceeding to Macedonia, led by what he correctly conjectured to be a call from God, he first settled at Philippi, and began to take measures for opening

* Acts xvi. 12—24.

his commission, and commencing the publication of the glad tidings. While daily passing from his lodging in the city, to a place of prayer at a little distance, " a certain damsel possessed with a spirit of divination, *which brought her masters much gain by soothsaying,*" frequently met him, and, openly following him and his company, cried, saying, " these men are the servants of the most high God, which show unto us the way of salvation." This woman, whose mind was disordered by something like the possessions mentioned in the Gospels, was supposed to be inspired by a divine spirit, and to be able, when excited, to foretell future events,—her masters, at least, so pretended to interpret her sayings as to give them the character of prophecy (or fortune-telling) and thus to make her an instrument of gain. Impelled, however, by an impulse which they did not understand, she was drawn habitually to approach the Apostles, and in the audience of observers to recognize and declare their extraordinary character,— just as the demons in Jerusalem and Judea, through the lips of the possessed, had acknowledged the Lord. " And this she did many days. But Paul, being grieved, turned and said to the spirit, I command thee in the name of Jesus Christ to come out of her. And he came out the same hour." The distracted and disordered intellect was healed. The woman was restored to her right mind, and was no longer an object of pity or aversion. Her countenance was calm, her eye clear, her deportment quiet, her speech rational. It was a sight that might have filled any heart with gladness and tears, and have led to eager and earnest enquiry into the object of the strangers in visiting the city, and the meaning of the damsel's mysterious words. But what did *they* care for goodness or truth who were partners in a sordid and mercenary speculation :—whose capital was invested in an expensive instrument,—who had no object but what was selfish,—who valued their slave, and lodged her, and fed her, only that they might use her for their pecuniary advantage, and whose "tender mercies" therefore "were cruel!" "When her masters saw that the hope of their gain was gone"— the Evil Spirit had *gone* from the damsel, and the "captive was delivered," but the prospect of gain was gone with it, and when they saw *that*—"they caught Paul and Silas, and drew them into the market-place unto the rulers." That nothing might be wanting to illustrate the bad influence of the love of lucre, their rage and disappointment developed into hypocrisy, and took the form of deeply-offended patriotism and religion! They brought them to the magistrates, saying, "These men, being Jews, do exceedingly trouble our city, and teach customs"—new forms of belief and worship—"which are not lawful for us to receive, being Romans." It is not necessary to pursue the story. It will be sufficient to say, that, from the resistance of Mammon in the minds of these men, to the light of truth and the kingdom of God, there resulted not only the rejection of "the way of salvation" for themselves, but the malignant persecution of the men who declared it. *They* had not "troubled the city," or caused any commotion; those who were exasperated by the loss of their "gains" did that! They excited the multitude, bullied the magistrates, raised a mob, and the result was, that the Apostles, as they themselves afterwards expressed it, "were shamefully entreated." Their clothes were torn off their backs; they were "beaten openly" with "many stripes;" were subjected to degradation, insolence, and insult, and at last were thrust into the common jail, and "their feet made fast in the stocks."

III.

The scene of the next fact, belonging to the third journey, is Ephesus.*

The incident occurred at the close of a lengthened residence of the Apostle in that city, and was occasioned by his ministerial success. The Gospel had been "so preached, that many believed." "All they that dwelt in Asia heard the word of the Lord Jesus." It penetrated the different classes of the

* Acts xix. 23—41.

community, and like leaven "was leavening the whole lump,"—"so mightily grew the word of God and prevailed." This provoked an attempt on the part of those "*whose craft was in danger*," and whose mercenary interests were thus imperilled, to withstand its influence, discourage its adherents, and check its progress. We refer to the well-known riot of Demetrius, the account of which we have in the Acts. The story is so admirably told,—the details are so minute, graphic and lifelike,—everything is in such perfect keeping, and stands forth with such an aspect of reality,—that we should only injure the impression which the simple perusal of the chapter will produce, if we attempted to put it into our own words. The movement of Demetrius, his speech to the craftsmen, the appeal skilfully made to their interest and *their religion;* the wrath evoked,—the shout and exclamation by which it was expressed; the excitement of the populace, their rushing into the theatre, the purpose of Paul to enter and face them (from which the prudence of his friends dissuaded him), the attempt of the Jews to clear themselves, their hope that "craftsmen" would listen to a "coppersmith," the reluctance of Alexander to be thrust forward, the torrent of opposition with which he was assailed, the "two hours'" shouting of a popular watchword, the ignorance of the mass as to what it all meant, the exhaustion at last of lungs and excitement, and the politic appeal of the town clerk; —every particular is so perfectly natural, that the entire picture stands before us like one of the most finished works of art,—admirable in grouping, in shading and colour, tone and touch,—what would have been recognized as the product of the inspiration of Genius, if it had not come to us in a book whose writers refer to " the inspiration of God."

The only point, however, that we have to do with is that which illustrates the matter in hand. Demetrius, the God-maker, was no fool. He was obviously a long-headed, sagacious man. The boldness with which he originated a reaction against the new beliefs, which were countenanced, if not professed, by many influential men; and the skill with which he went to work in enlisting the hostility and inflaming the fanaticism of the interested artificers; shew him to have been a person of vigor and ability. We can hardly imagine that he himself had any very earnest belief in the divinity of the images which his men manufactured; or that his jealous concern for the established orthodoxy was not stimulated by past profits and prospective loss. He might have heard the Apostle preach; he must have heard of the wonders attributed to him; he certainly knew of the moral influence which his teaching exerted,—" that not alone in Ephesus, but almost throughout all Asia, Paul had persuaded and turned away much people, saying that they were no Gods that were made with hands." Had his craft not been in danger, he was just the man who would have vindicated his independence by thoroughly examining into the facts of the case. *His money-interests* impeded and checked the actings of his intellect, fettered its freedom, or even perhaps, rendered the slightest movement, or desire to move, towards the neighbourhood of the new truth, a moral impossibility. Demetrius was a far more respectable personage than Elymas the sorcerer, or the owners of the poor girl at Philippi. There is no necessity for supposing that he was fully or consciously aware of the motives which influenced him in what he did. If the word "truth" had been written on a piece of paper lying before him, but with one of his silver shrines lying upon *it*, he certainly would not have been able to read the word; and, if anything was said about its being there, he might positively affirm that *he could not see it.* Of course he could not. The discovery could only come from the removal of the "shrine,"—the interposing substance between the eye and the object. So, as long as the first thought of the man was "*that* is my living,—by that 'we have our wealth,' consideration, personal comfort, social respectability,—I cannot give up that,"—so long Truth itself would be hidden from him by very necessity, and he might even believe himself to be

E

sincerely persuaded of its *not* being near him. We must not be too hard upon Demetrius and the craftsmen. Their type of character grows up so naturally, in every age and in all countries, in the neighbourhood of any established or traditional faith, that, instead of indulging in condemnation, we had better institute inquiry; instead of glorying over them, let us suspect ourselves; there is always occasion enough amongst us, in respect to something or other, for each to adopt the question of the disciples, " Lord, is it I ? " —" Am I falling into the sin of Demetrius ? Is there any form in which worldly interest comes in between me and thee ?—is it eclipsing the light of truth, or disturbing the aspect of duty, or repressing salutary doubt, or hindering the entrance of conviction ? " Or, to keep more expressly to the analogy of the case, the question might be, " Am I so absorbed by the interests of business, and so jealous of whatever might endanger my success, that my ears are closed to the call of God, and my eyes to the light of the objects of faith ? Does the thought of these things, or the advocacy of their claim, when earnest and pointed, instead of being welcome, rather vex and irritate, and provoke to something like active resistance ? "

IV.

This enumeration of illustrative facts, taken from

the Gospel narratives and the Apostolic history, may be closed by a statement from the writings of St. Paul, which also refers to *a matter of fact;* a fact historically true, he says,—not indeed, in relation to any specifically named individual, or individuals, but in respect to a class : a statement which would seem to receive its best significance, by being regarded as illustrative of the influence of Mammon-worship, or worldly-mindedness, in so darkening and indurating the soul as to obstruct the approach to it of religious light. The statement occurs in the second letter to the Corinthians, iv. 2—4. " Seeing we have this ministry, as we have received mercy, we faint not; but have renounced the hidden things of dishonesty, not walking in craftiness, nor handling the Word of God deceitfully; but by manifestation of the truth commending ourselves to every man's conscience in the sight of God."—What a conviction, by the way, the man who thus wrote must have had of his own disinterestedness;—his freedom from base motives, his being actuated by nothing but the love of truth, and the utmost singleness and purity of purpose. What a contrast he presents to the several men who have been passing before us; and how natural it was for him to say, on another occasion, " our exhortation to you was not of deceit, nor in guile; neither at any time used we flattering words, as ye know; nor a cloak of covetousness; God is witness."—One seems to feel that such a man has a right to speak as he goes on to do, though it involves a severe judgment on the mental condition and actuating motives of others,—a region into which it always becomes us to fear to penetrate. "If our Gospel be hid"—if men complain that they cannot see it, that it does not approve itself to them,—" It is hid to them that are lost." To them, that is to say, who are *being* lost, who are in the process of perishing, who are going *towards* that destruction which men bring upon themselves by their impenitence and unbelief. "If our Gospel be hid, it is hid to them who are self-destroyed;"—in respect to whom, "*the God of this world* hath blinded the minds of them that believe not,"—blinded them, "*lest* the light of the glorious Gospel of Christ, who is the image of God, should shine into them." The God of this world, the principle of earthlymindedness, is here represented as a bad intelligence, as a malignant Personal Agent, acting on men with design and aim, —with a deliberately selected bad object,—blinding the mind, *lest* the light of the Gospel " should shine into it." Mammon, you see, *in* a man, will so scheme and plan as to keep God out. What a contrast there is between the gross, palpable obscure, penetrating and investing the mind of those under the influence of the God of this world, and the description that follows of *their* condition out of whom the world has been cast, and the gates of whose hearts have been lifted up, that "the king of Glory might come in:"—"*God who commanded the light to shine out of darkness, hath shined in our hearts, to give the light of the knowledge of the glory of God, in the face of Jesus Christ.*"

Sermon III.

MARK iv. 19.

"The cares of this world, the deceitfulness of riches, and the lusts of other things, choke the word, and it becometh unfruitful."

HAVING largely illustrated the opposition of Mammon to *the entrance* of light and truth into the soul, we proceed to exhibit some of the many ways in which it is represented as exercising an antagonist influence to the Divine life *after it has begun*.

We shall start from the first indications of a desire to receive, or a willingness to welcome the word of the kingdom, as shewn by attention to the truth, or the outward profession of it. Advancing from primary impressions and convictions, we shall notice cases in which such impressions become apparently fixed, and such convictions develope and expand till years are spent in connexion with the Church, and even in the discharge of some of its higher official functions. In doing this, we shall have to shew how the money-lust operates disastrously at every stage and in all cir-

THE GOOD SEED CHOKED.

cumstances. How it stifles the voice of conscience, checks the awakening of the soul, cools the ardour of zeal, leads to inconsistencies of behaviour, induces apostacy from the faith, corrupts the ministry, depraves the people, and is the fruitful source of incalculable evils. All along, from beginning to end, the "unrighteous" and malignant "Mammon" is wakeful and active. If it cannot prevent the beginnings of religion, it will watch its cradle, and seek its life; if it cannot destroy it then, it may be seen afterwards to follow and dog the steps of the faithful, to seek to cripple or seduce, and in many instances to appear to succeed. The bones of its victims lie whitening in the sun on both sides of "the narrow way," eloquent though silent monitors to all in every age who profess to be "pilgrims and strangers on the earth;"—who say that they are seeking "another country, even an heavenly,"—"a city which hath foundations,"—where they have "laid up their treasure," "the true riches," and where, consequently, "their heart is," and they themselves are longing to be!

We begin by noticing some things that occur in the Gospels, which, more or less, fall in with the earlier stages of the course referred to.

Two of the classes of hearers included in the parable of the Sower, may be taken as illustrations of the love of the world frustrating incipient religious impressions. These are the "stony ground" hearers, and those in whom the seed "fell among thorns." The one welcomed the word with joy; they stood forth, and showed gaily and bravely for a while; but when persecution was to be faced, and sacrifices made, "they were offended," and immediately "fell away." This was the work of Mammon,—in the form of the love of ease, or of reputation, or of life, or of worldly possessions. The love of God had not so entered into and filled the heart, as to cast out the love of the world, and to inspire a heroic and disinterested courage. Of the other class our Lord himself says, that the thorns which grew up and choked the word, so that no fruit was brought to perfection, were "the cares of this world—the deceitfulness of riches—and the lusts of other things." Mammon, that is to say, in diversified manifestation,—excessive and sinful secular solicitude, the sunshine and seductions of worldly success, the greed and exorbitancy of irregular desire.

The evil influence of low aims, mixed motives, and mere worldly or political ambition, may be seen in various ways breaking out in those who professed to be our Lord's disciples. In the many, for instance, who hailed him as a prophet, and appeared to welcome and submit themselves to his teaching; and even at times in the favoured few, who were his chosen associates and familiar friends. The proof of this consists in many noticeable things, all more or less indicating the secret suggestions of the World and Mammon. To this must be referred the conduct of those who followed Jesus from place to place, seemed interested in his teaching and impressed by his miracles—and who perhaps were so, to a certain extent—but in whom the strongest thing was, the memory of the distribution of the loaves and fishes, and the hope of witnessing the wonder again! Whatever impressions might have been made upon such persons, it was perfectly natural that they should "walk no more with him," when he advanced to his higher religious lessons, and gave to "bread" and "flesh" a spiritual significance. But among more noticeable men—men in prominent public positions —there were those, it would seem, who in their consciences admitted the claims of Jesus, but whose convictions were over-ruled by worldly considerations so that no correspondent result followed. The good seed died in the ground. Hence we read, that "Among the chief rulers also many believed on him; but because of the Pharisees they did not confess him, lest they should be put out of the synagogue; for they loved the praise of men more than the praise of God."

But even among those who neither "went back" nor hesitated to "confess" him—the members themselves of the Apostolic family who professed to cleave to Him " because he had the words of eternal life "—how often, and how flagrantly, even in *them*, did the " briars and thorns," naturally belonging to the soil of their imperfectly purified nature, keep cropping out in their words and actions! There was something of this in those swellings of pride, that perilous inflation, which followed the exercise of their miraculous endowments:—there was something of it, too, when they forbad others to do a mighty work because " they followed not with *them;* " and there was a great deal of it, when, displeased with some Samaritans, they wished to be permitted " to bring down fire from heaven to consume them!" In all this, there was the influence of Mammon seeking to stifle and " choke " the early springing up of the good seed;—his influence, not, indeed, in the form of the love of money, but in that of the love of distinction, of noticeable superiority,—"the honour that cometh from men." Something perhaps *lower* than this lurked in the question of what *they* were to get, as an equivalent for the act which they paraded by saying, " Lo! *we* have left all and followed thee; "—something *similar*, both in the ambition of those who wished to sit on the right hand and the left of the Lord when he should receive the kingdom and reign as king; and in the indignation of the rest who were angry with their brethren for trying to get the start of them, by clandestinely procuring a promise for themselves. The same spirit, not yet cast out—always reluctant to leave the heart, and never leaving it without strenuous, and sometimes long conflict with its divine antagonist—appears in the contentions which so frequently arose among the Apostles as to "which of them should be the greatest;"—in the tenacity with which they clung to the idea of a national Messiah and a political redemption, evinced by their inability to understand our Lord's words when he spake of his approaching death, and in their actually "rebuking" him for thus speaking, and rejecting the thought as an utter incredibility;—in their weakness and terror when the end came;—and in the darkness and despair that settled upon them when they thought that all was lost,—the visions they had indulged being buried with *him* whom "they *had trusted was he who should have redeemed Israel;*"—and, still further, in the revival within them of their old Jewish ambition, when their hopes were reanimated by the assurance of his resurrection, so that one of the last questions they put to him was prompted by this, rather than by any exalted *Christian* aspirations, "Lord, wilt thou at this time *restore again the kingdom to Israel?*" In all these things, and in others that might be mentioned, there is indicated to us how the darkness of nature and the God of this world struggled against light and life—the true light and the new life—in the first period of their actings and influence in the hearts of the favoured and distinguished twelve—the Lord's elected and ordained Apostles! The traffickers and money-changers that infested the temple had to be ejected by force; but after ejectment they returned again, and again settled themselves in the sacred precincts. There might be a mystic significance in this fact, recorded to illustrate the character of the adversary, the spirit of Mammon, which, in one form or other, has to be cast out of every living temple, but which still lingers and hovers about it bent on finding an opportunity to return.*

Leaving, however, these apparently slight but really serious and suggestive indications of the unconscious working of the spirit of evil in good men, during the first stage of their better life; we will bring before you two or three examples of a darker character, in which, after more or less of mental excitement and religious profession, the "unrighteous Mammon" achieves a signal and disastrous success.

I.

We begin with the case of Felix.† It is admitted that he might have been referred to as illustrating

* Mark iv. 19; John vi. 26—66; John xiv. 42, 43; Luke x. 17; Luke ix. 49, 54; Math. xix. 27; Mark x. 35—41; Mark ix. 33, 34. Math. xvi. 22; Math. xxvi. 56. Luke xxiv. 21; Acts i. 6; John ii. 13, with Math. xxi. 12.
† Acts xxiv. 24—27.

how a worldly and wicked state of heart obstructs a man's reception of the kingdom of God; but looked at more narrowly, it will be seen, that he may be especially regarded as exemplifying the influence of the love of money in overcoming convictions, and in hardening the conscience against their return.

Partly, perhaps, from something of curiosity in himself, and partly to gratify that of Drusilla, he appointed a meeting with Paul to hear him "concerning the faith of Christ." Paul's knowledge of the man and his natural power of adapting his address to all sorts of auditors— directed by the assistance of that Spirit whose guiding help was especially promised at such times—enabled him so to "reason of righteousness, temperance, and judgment to come" that "Felix trembled." The arrow entered into his soul;—conscience was aroused, memory awakened, apprehension evoked,—the past affrighted and the future appalled him. He did not ridicule, or scoff, or oppose, or contradict. He was morally and deeply affected,—at once excited and subdued. The Spirit by which Paul spake gave to his argument a penetrating power, and threw it into the soul with a living force. The man trembled and *might have been saved*. Those tremors and convictions of his, had they been obeyed, might have issued in penitence and faith, and been to him the beginning of the life of God! But he sought an immediate, though temporary solace, in an excuse as irrational as it was fallacious, and so transparently a subterfuge, that it could hardly, one would think, have deceived himself. He would "call" for Paul again, "when he had a more convenient season!"—as if he had not arranged that very meeting for the express purpose of listening to him. He trembled and might have been saved; but—*he procrastinated and was lost.*

What is specially to be noted, however, in connexion with our present subject, is the man's subsequent behaviour. Felix was corrupt and unprincipled, because he was voluptuous;—he was extravagant in his expenditure, because he denied himself nothing; he wanted money to support his extravagance. " The love of money is the root of all evil." Not that it prompts to all in each individual—for if the soul be absorbed by it, it may act as an antagonist to other sins; there are vices from which the purely covetous are necessarily free. But the love of money is the root of all evil, because it may underlie and be connected with the indulgence of all bad propensities whatsoever;—it becomes the associate of every other lust, and resolves itself into the love of every thing "earthly, sensual, devilish" that money can be employed to purchase. Felix loved money, not as an ultimate end, but as a necessary instrument; and in this form it stifled his conscience, hardened his heart, and destroyed his soul. There is nothing, perhaps, in all history, so deliberately base and wicked as this man's conduct after his momentarily quickened spirit relapsed into indifference, and sunk down within him "twice dead." *"He hoped also that money should have been given him of Paul, that he might loose him: wherefore he sent for him the oftener, and communed with him."* The folly of this is as enormous as its wickedness, illustrating the truth that the greatest sinners are often the greatest fools. The idea of imagining that a man who had "reasoned" like Paul "of righteousness, and temperance, and judgment to come" would be found to be in himself so hypocritical and so base, as to be capable of giving a bribe, and of "striking hands" in a partnership of iniquity! The hardihood of his venturing to suggest such a thing,—the deliberate wickedness of again and again sending for him, to "commune with him," as it would seem, about "the faith of Christ," but only to drop hints of his mercenary object! An attempt to corrupt Paul! It is not to be wondered at, that though he thus found many a "convenient season" for converse with the Apostle, he never trembled more! The motions of the Spirit never visited him again. It was perfectly natural that, baffled and disappointed in his hope of "base gain," he should, in going out of office, "leave Paul bound," —not because he thought it right, or had not the power to liberate him, but because he was "willing," from a selfish motive, "to do the Jews a pleasure."

II.

We advance a step further in the next case; in which, however, we have to do rather with a surprized intellect, than an awakened conscience. We refer to Simon Magus.* This man was one of the same class with Elymas the sorcerer, whom Paul encountered at Paphos, and with those "vagabond Jews" whom you find acting as "exorcists" at Ephesus. He was distinguished by extraordinary proficiency in the tricks and arts common to them all. He was, no doubt, a man of cleverness and ability, for without considerable resources of intelligence and skill he could never have produced the impression he did on the minds of the Samaritans. When the Evangelist Philip "went down" to the city of Samaria "and preached Christ unto them," he came across Simon in the height of his popularity. The people were "bewitched" by him, and had been so for a long time. Philip, however, not only spoke to them of far higher and more penetrating themes than Simon, but his word was accompanied by such visible wonders, in the form of supernatural attestation, as they had never witnessed before. "When," therefore, "they believed Philip preaching the things

* Acts viii. 5—24.

concerning the kingdom of God, and the name of Jesus Christ, they were baptized, both men and women." Simon was taken by surprise; he was defeated where he had thought to reign; he was astonished at once by the means and the results. His adherents fell away. The multitude melted from around him. Nor was there wanting to account for it loftier argument than his, and works and wonders more manifestly indicating "The great power of God." "Then Simon himself believed also: and when he was baptized, he continued with Philip, and wondered, *beholding the miracles and signs which were done.*" There is nothing here of stir and excitement in the moral faculties; trembling and apprehension from the thought of "righteousness and temperance and judgment to come." The probability is, that Simon was less affected by what Philip taught of "the things concerning the kingdom of God," than by what he did in confirmation of his message. In some way or other, however, he was so influenced and overcome, that he professed to believe in Christ;—it is said, indeed, that he did believe, and on the profession of that belief, "was baptized."

Like Milton's angel, who, even in heaven, was always far more intent on its golden pavement, its rich and precious gems, than in sympathy with its ideas, services and song, Simon, transformed into a disciple of Philip, had his thoughts busied, as we have intimated, not with the spiritual truths of which he heard, but with the signs and wonders which he saw. There can be no doubt that he looked at them in the spirit of his profession; kept calculating in thought how much he could make if he had Philip's marvellous ability, and how much he *should* make when he had discovered his secret, to find out which, was probably his object in becoming a disciple. While this was going on, two other men appeared on the scene— Peter and John—whose power over occult agencies seemed as far to surpass Philip's as Philip's was felt by Simon to surpass his own. Philip could do wonders, but he could not impart to others the power to do them. But when Peter and John laid their hands on the baptized converts, "they received the Holy Ghost;" and, as the proof of this consisted in something external, something which could be perceived by others, we are to understand, as in similar cases, that "they spake with tongues," and "magnified God;"—magnified God, that is, they gave utterance, in their own tongue, to their new spiritual conceptions with the pomp, elevation, and copiousness of inspired verse. When Simon *saw* this, he could no longer conceal the secret motive by which he had all along been influenced. He had wished to acquire Philip's proficiency by getting at his secret: but here was a power higher still, which, if he could attain, he should of course succeed in his first object—for the greater would include the less, the power to *confer* extraordinary gifts would involve the power to exercise them. The possession of this would be worth anything. Whatever it might cost, the use that could be made of it would very soon repay that. Dazzled by the prospect, Simon lost all prudential restraint over his mercenary spirit; he let out not only his hitherto concealed personal object, but that he thought each of the apostles " altogether such an one as himself!"— cleverer indeed, but equally animated by the love of gain, and open to any good pecuniary offer! " When he saw that through laying on of the Apostle's hands the Holy Ghost was given, *he offered them money,* saying, give me also this power, that on whomsoever I lay hands, he may receive the Holy Ghost." The suggestion was perfectly appalling. It shocked and confounded Peter and John, and stirred them up to something like vituperative indignation. Indeed, if it was bad in Felix to try to get Paul to *give* him a bribe to purchase his liberty, it was far worse in Simon to *offer* one to Peter and John as a price for such a power as they were requested to confer. " But Peter said unto him, thy money perish with thee, because thou hast thought that the gift of God may be purchased with money. Thou hast neither part nor lot in this matter; for thy heart is not right in the sight of God. Repent therefore of this thy wickedness, and pray God, if perhaps the thought of thine heart may be forgiven thee. For I perceive that thou art in the gall of bitterness, and in the bond of iniquity." So hardening to the heart, so darkening to the intellect, was the passion for money as thus seen in Simon. In spite of belief, baptism, profession, his spiritual nature was never touched; his moral feeling never awakened. Selfish and personal objects—thoughts of honour and wealth—were all that moved him. He never apprehended the importance of truth, felt the reality of sin, realized his relations to God, or hoped for or desired His salvation. All within him was dark, cold, calculating, base. And it remained so to the last. In his heartless reply to Peter's terrible words, there is no allusion to his "wickedness" and "iniquity," but only to his peril; no expression of penitence, no sigh of contrition, no anxiety for that possible forgiveness which he so much needed, but only a low selfish solicitude for personal safety:— "pray ye to the Lord for me, *that none of these things which ye have spoken come upon me.*"

III.

The next case will take us a step farther than the last, as that took us a step farther than the previous one. In what is now to be noticed, we have no particulars of personal experience; we have neither the moral excitement of Felix, nor the immoral intellectual excitement of Simon; but we have the facts of discipleship, and of standing in the church, and of social position which give to the illustration about to be referred to, very peculiar pregnancy and suggestiveness. With this remark we introduce the case of Ananias and Sapphira.* The incident recorded respecting these persons, tho' happening in an age of prodigies may be looked at apart from that; and then it will be found to have lessons in it, remarkably applicable and pointedly admonitory to an age with such religious characteristics as our own.

Ananias and Sapphira were among the early fruits of the Apostolic Ministry after the descent of the Spirit, and were numbered among the disciples who constituted the first Christian Church. They might have been present on the day of Pentecost, and been witnesses of its wonders;—they saw, perhaps, "the cloven tongues like as of fire" which sat on the heads of the Apostles, and heard the words of Peter and were "pricked" by them in their heart. Or they might have been in the temple, and seen "the impotent man"—to whom they might sometimes have given alms—after being healed by Peter, "walking and leaping, and praising God;" and, there, drawn towards the Apostle when he addressed the multitude, they might have listened to his exhortation, and felt his word come to them in power. Or they might

* Acts v. 1—11.

have been induced to accept the new truth, from being brought into personal contact with it through the influence and persuasion of relatives or friends, and so were among one or other of those accessions of disciples whom the Lord "daily added to the Church." But, however this might be, *in* the Church they were. They had professedly accepted the Apostolic message; had been baptized probably by Apostolic hands; and might have occasionally received the apostles under their roof, as they were then in the habit of "breaking bread from house to house." Ananias and Sapphira were in the Church when there broke out that extraordinary and affluent gushing of affection—that utter forgetfulness of self—under the new feeling of Christian brotherhood, which "made them that believed to be of one heart and of one soul," so that, "neither said any of them that the things which he possessed were his own; but they had all things common." This went so far, that "as many as were possessors of lands or houses sold them, and brought the prices of the things that were sold, and laid them down at the Apostles' feet."

Now the precise point to be noted here is, that this relinquishment of property, this scale of contribution to the common fund, involving all that a man possessed, was no divine appointment; it rested on no new revelation, or on any Apostolic law; it was binding on no one; and might have been disregarded without sin. From Peter's words about it we learn, that a man's property "was his own" to keep or sell, devote or not, as he pleased; that even if he went so far as to turn lands into money with a view of giving it to the Church, if he repented of his purpose, or altered his judgment, he was at liberty to do so; the money like the land was "in his own power." All was voluntary; no one compelled. Here, however, comes out the very pith of the lesson with which the incident is fraught. There was no law imposing payment and specifying amount; but there was a public opinion and a general practice that took its place. There was an impulse and an enthusiasm, which you would be singular if you did not obey and share. There was a fashion, so to speak (using the word without prejudice), which you would be marked or *talked of*, if you did not conform to. This was a severe test to weak natures;—especially if there were combined in such, a wish to stand well in the society with a desire to retain their wealth; or a perfectly allowable difference of judgment as to the mode or amount of contribution. This mixed feeling indeed is what constitutes the weakness of the weak. Ananias and Sapphira were affected by it. They were swayed by contradictory impulses, and in trying to obey both, they fell. The probability is, that both the motives that influenced them were bad, and that their characters would not have been bettered, tho' their exposure would have been prevented, had they entirely yielded themselves to one;—that is, had they either given up their property, all, absolutely and without reserve; or if they had retained it, and given nothing;—or given openly and professedly a limited donation and no more.

They had not strength to follow out either the one or the other of these courses. Attempting a compromise—a middle path, by which they were to get more reputation than they deserved, and to part with less of their property than they pretended—they of course fell into "the snare of the Devil, and were taken captive by him at his will." They sold their property, and got the credit of doing so; it might be a public act, or they took care to let it be publicly known. But they could not bring themselves to part with all the purchase money; they did not like to leave themselves without some reserved pecuniary stay. But their professions had committed them and they were ashamed to draw back; or rather, indeed, they *wished* the repute of magnanimous liberality without paying the price at which it was to be bought. Either way, they "agreed together" to act a lie, and to tell one if necessary. They made the attempt "to serve God and Mammon;"—to honour the one and yet to hold with the other; to seem to sacrifice everything to the Church as an act of love, henceforth professedly to live by faith; but storing away as their visible confidence a cruse of oil and barrel of meal that should not fail. It was the "unrighteous Mammon" that whispered the promise; they gave him the trust which they withdrew from God; the consequence was such as evinced at once the "deceitfulness" of the idol and the folly of his worshippers.

The manner in which Ananias and Sapphira were detected and punished is striking and admonitory, not so much for its display of apostolic power, as for its revelation of the greatness of their sin. That sin consisted in their pretence and hypocrisy; in their wish to secure reputation, on the ground of great liberality and personal sacrifice, without either the one or the other; in their want of faith, evinced by their conforming, or appearing to conform, to a high standard of pecuniary contribution, while their secret and concealed provision for themselves gave the lie to their outward acts, and developed into an open and uttered lie to God. And these people were professed Christians,—fellow communicants with evangelists and Apostles,—witnesses of the miracles, and attendants on the ministry of inspired men! They were under no obligation, as we have already intimated, to do what they pretended to have done. They were not bound to follow the example of others,—to imitate the zeal and equal the donations of their fellow disciples, if they could not do so with all their heart,—with the approval of their reason, and as the expression of a spontaneous and spiritual impulse. They not only had not moral courage enough to follow their own judgment,—which might have exposed them to remark, tho' it might have been no sin; but they were tempted to aspire to a reputation for liberality, while their love of money as an object of trust, led them to try to deceive men and to dissemble with God. Their fate is recorded as a solemn warning for all time;—as an eloquent admonition to every Christian man to be true and transparent, upright and conscientious, especially in professed sacrifices for God. Their sin was their own; their punishment was for us. They were struck down "before all," that others also might fear. They seem to say to us,—'"be not deceived; God is not mocked; he that soweth to the flesh, shall of the flesh reap corruption." God loveth an upright, as well as a "cheerful giver." "The cup of cold water" in the spirit of a disciple is of more value than houses and lands in the spirit of the world,—the offering of ostentation, or the extorted gift of an unwelcome necessity,—especially so, if, while professing to give all to God, you keep a reserve as a sacrifice to Mammon and to self.'

IV.

These three illustrative instances of the terrible results of the love of money, in counteracting the influence of the power of Truth, may suffice for the present. They present different aspects of the one bad and baneful principle which pervades them all. In Felix, the love of money as the instrument of procuring animal indulgence, arrests the convictions of conscience, stupifies the soul, and prompts to acts the most mean and despicable, as well as wicked. In Simon Magus it paralyses the understanding; it blinds the man to the meaning of words, the significance of true "signs," the eloquence of a holy life. It permits intellectual surprise and wonder, but unites them with indifference to all that would touch the moral faculty, and excite and guide the aspirations of the spirit. It prompts to an outward religious profession, and submission to a religious rite, for the mere purpose or with the secret hope of making good the calculations of cupidity. It hides from its victim the true and the real in earnest and sincere men; and culminates in the betrayal of his own hollowness, by leading him to speak and act on the presumption that others were just as bad as himself. In Ananias and Sapphira, the same principle comes into play in another form, and in a more advanced ecclesiastical condition. Felix is brought into contact with truth, and experiences its power; Simon goes further and enrolls himself among catechumens and enquirers; Ananias and Sapphira are beyond this, and come before us as accepted and recognized Christian people. They have a history, and a standing, and a character as such. In them, as we have seen, the love of the world—the clinging to and trusting in that treasure "which men may lay up for themselves on earth"—is manifested in a form of complicated malignity. Deliberate agreement between man and wife to perpetrate a great sin; ostentation, hypocrisy, fraud, falsehood, and other suggestions and devices of the Devil are successively evolved, till, with an uplifted face, a steady countenance, and an unfaltering voice they utter their lie to that Holy Spirit which rested on and ruled in Apostolic men! People look for the proof of human depravity in the world at large. The most flagrant and fearful proofs of it are to be found in the Church. It will be well for us all to lay to heart the alarm of Isaiah, and the lamentation of Christ;— "Let the sinners in Zion be afraid, let fearfulness surprise the hypocrites. Judgment will I lay to the line, and righteousness to the plummet; and the hail shall sweep away the refuge of lies, and the waters shall overflow the hiding-place. And your covenant with death shall be annulled, and your agreement with hell shall not stand; when the overflowing scourge shall pass through, then shall ye be trodden down by it."—"Woe unto thee Chorazin, woe unto thee Bethsaida; for if the mighty works which have been done in you, had been done in Tyre and Sidon, they would have repented in dust and ashes, and have remained unto this day." "The men of Nineveh shall rise up against this generation and shall condemn it; for they repented at the preaching of Jonas, and behold! a greater than Jonas is here." Responsibility is in proportion to advantage; sin is aggravated by privilege and profession. Children of the light, if their deeds are evil, are worse than those who are still wandering in darkness. "If I had not come a light into the world, ye had not had sin, but now ye have no cloak for your sin." "If ye were blind ye should have no sin; but now ye say *we see*, therefore your sin remaineth!"—

Let us conclude by all joining in the prayers of David, each making them his own. "Open thou mine eyes." "Teach me thy statutes." "Unite my heart to love thy law," and "fear thy name." "Search me, and try me, O God, and see if there be any wicked way in me, and lead me in the way everlasting."

Sermon IV.

1 Timothy vi. 10.

"The love of money is the root of all evil."

IN our last discourse we referred at some length to the cases of Felix, Simon Magus, and Ananias and Sapphira, as all illustrating, with specific differences, the bad influence of the love of money. We saw how it affected the convictions of the conscience, the perceptions of the intellect, and the general phenomena of the religious life. The subject in hand has been so advanced by the last two cases, that we are now in the midst of the Christian community. We shall henceforth have to deal with the evils of covetousness as we may find them exhibited in the members and ministers of the first churches. Ananias and Sapphira were private members of the church at Jerusalem. Simon Magus was ambitious of being an apostle; he wanted to be endowed with the highest powers of the highest office. We purpose, this morning, to collect and classify the different statements in the New Testament in relation to correspondent matters of fact—the actual corruption of Christian character, and the enormities in ministerial conduct, which, in the age, and under the very eye of the apostles, were seen to flow from the love of money, "the root of all evil."

I am sorry to say it, but I have been surprised to find that by far the worst representations in the New Testament of this aspect of the subject, and the most numerous, belong to those who were teachers, preachers, and ministers in the church; and that some of the most revolting and terrible of the prophetic pictures of the future, the apostolic announcements of what was to come, are concerned with what would be called, in ordinary language, the baseness, corruption, and degeneracy of the clergy. It is hardly possible, indeed, to find any of the darker strokes of the Apostolic pencil, in depicting either what was then in the church or what time was to develope, which is not preceded or followed by allusions to official persons;—to those whom some would designate "the Christian *priesthood.*"

I.

We begin, however, by quoting one or two passages which may be regarded as applying to private members of the Christian community. We take the first from the neighbourhood of the text, including the statements before and after. "*They that will be rich* fall into temptation and a snare, and into many foolish and hurtful lusts, which drown men in destruction and perdition. *For the love of money is ·the root of all evil; which while some coveted after, they have erred from the faith, and pierced themselves through with many sorrows."* These are terrible words. They set before us what may be the perilous results to a Christian man, of his giving way to the desire and determination to be rich. They are spoken of *Christians*—for some of the evils enumerated could only occur in the case of such. The covetous wish, when retained and encouraged, and especially the mercenary resolve, blinds a man to the niceties of practical morality; his feet give way, his plans get crooked and his principles get debauched; he "falls into temptation," and so gets caught and "ensnared" by pursuing some questionable course, or joining in some unwarrantable venture. As the mind gets worldly, the affections become corrupt. As the leadings of the Spirit are resisted and refused; as the light within wanes and darkens; the heart opens "to foolish and fleshly lusts." Success engenders vanity and pride, and prompts to extravagance and display. Or failure has to be concealed and losses recovered by keeping up appearances, or by other arts which involve deceit,—than which nothing so deadens the moral sensibility, or more surely leads to the playing of a desperate game. Or stimulants are had recourse to, that the man may lose himself for a while under stupefaction or excitement. The result is, that success or failure may alike involve the destruction of the character, and the perdition of the soul. The world in the heart darkens the mind to the beauty and purity of Divine truth, so that errors of faith frequently follow from obliquities of conduct. "Evil communications" corrupt alike good morals and spiritual religion. Conformity to the world, or intercourse with questionable society, often ends in conformity of opinion. Revealed truth seems less sacred, Scriptural holiness less obligatory; the result is, a drifting away from what was once believed, professed and reverenced; till, waking up to the melancholy change, or not waking but yet suffering the consequences, the man finds himself "pierced through with many sorrows;"—sorrows round about him like so many darts sticking in and lacerating his whole body; or like so many sharp and poisoned arrows which have penetrated to the vitals, round which the flesh has tightened and closed, so that neither can the shafts be drawn out, nor the wounds mollified.

Another passage of like import, though still more specifically expressive of what is gross and offensive in character, occurs in the Epistle to the Philippians iii. 18, 19—"Many walk of whom I have told you often, and now tell you even weeping, that they are the enemies of the cross of Christ: whose end is destruction, whose God is their belly, and whose glory is in their shame; *who mind earthly things."* These persons were professed Christians; members of and communicants in the Church. Instead, however, of being "spiritually minded," and "setting their affections on things above," as becomes those who, "risen with Christ," have to aspire towards the world where He is;—instead of this, they are represented as being utterly "*earthly* minded;" as affecting and affected by "earthly things;" feeling and acting as if they thought themselves "debtors to the flesh to live after the flesh." This earthly mindedness was the central and radical element of their character, and the natural source of what practically distinguished them. Hence their subjection to animal satisfactions, their deification, so to speak, of mere appetite;—"their God is their belly:" and their exulting in the low liberty they exercised, as if it were conferred by a new revelation :—" they gloried in their shame." The consequence was, that this being connected with a Christian profession, they became "*the enemies of the cross of Christ.*" The expression is singularly suggestive. Men of earthly minds and base habits were enemies—not merely to the divine beauty of the character of Jesus, the purity of His precepts, and the sanctities of the world which He had revealed, but—*to the cross.* In those days, Christ was Christianity and the cross Christ. "He died for our sins." To redeem, indeed, and deliver from the penalty of transgression, but also that He might be the death of sin; might condemn it in the flesh; emancipate from its thraldom; raise humanity above its seductions and its indulgence; and, through the power of the fact that "He was made sin," might make for and "purify to himself a peculiar people zealous of good works." All this—the objective fact and its declared purpose—the men before us professed to believe. For *them*, therefore, to be what they were, in character and life, was to place themselves in direct antagonism to the cross:—to the central truth of that Gospel, which, while " bringing salvation," " teacheth the denying of all ungodliness and worldly lusts, and the living soberly and righteously in the world." To live differently, while professing to be His, is " to make Christ the minister of sin." Thus, His worst foes are the inconsistent and unfaithful of His own house. This, these men were. The beginning of their fall was their " minding earthly things;"—the "end," as in the former case, was to be " destruction" and perdition.

Another passage may be referred to as illustrating how the moral and spiritual tone of a man's mind may get lowered by too keen a pursuit of business, with a view to making a fortune. It is not wrong for a religious man to be a thoroughly devoted, farseeing, clever man of business; nor is it wrong for him to lay plans and engage in enterprises "to make money," in the usual meaning of that phrase. But it *is* wrong for him so to toil, and purpose, and speculate, as if he were independent of God;—as if he could carry out his schemes and secure success without *Him;*—as if a Christian might "use lightness" and "purpose in the flesh," and reckon on results without reference to the Divine blessing,—without remembering that "he knoweth not what a day may bring forth," and that it is "God who gives" both the opportunity and "the power to get wealth." This earthly and atheistic spirit, which leads men to act as if they had excluded God from the government of His own world, or at least from all interference with the ordinary concerns of life, is fostered by the absorbing pursuit of gain, and especially by the consciousness of business talents, long-headed sagacity, and uniform success. This spirit, it would seem, made its appearance in some of the Christian believers of the Apostolic age,—men in a large way of business, who took long journeys, and trafficked in the merchandise of many lands. Hence says St. James, (4 ch. 13 v.) "*Go to now, ye who say to-day or to-morrow we will go into such a city, and continue there a year, and buy and sell and get gain;* whereas ye know not what shall be on the morrow. For what is your life? It is even as a vapour, that appeareth for a little time and then vanisheth away. For that ye ought to say, if the Lord will we shall live and do this or that. But now ye rejoice in your boastings; all such rejoicing is evil."

II.

These passages may be regarded as referring to Christians in general, to those who were in the church as ordinary members; though it is not to be denied, that even of these passages, the first two rather glance side-ways at official men. Leaving that, however, we will now notice several statements which show how the love of money—a sordid and mercenary spirit—had debased and corrupted the minds of many in the Apostolic churches, who were, or who pretended to be, *teachers and ministers of the word.*

Such passages as the following indicate this— Titus i. 10, "There are many unruly and vain talkers and deceivers, whose mouths must be stopped, who subvert whole houses, *teaching things which they ought not for filthy lucre's sake.*" That statement is plain enough. There is no disguising or mincing the matter there. It is true that the Apostle says that, in this description, he refers "especially to some of the circumcision;" but, in the first place, the very phrase implies that he does not refer *exclusively* to them; and, in the second place, it is to be remembered, that the "circumcision" meant not Jews simply, but Jewish Christians;—men of whom there were thousands in Jerusalem recognized by the Apostles as legitimately belonging to the Church; who believed in Christ, but who were still zealous for the law. It was in their character as teachers of the new faith, that they turned it into an instrument for making money, and "taught things which they ought not for filthy lucre's sake."

2 Tim. iii. 6, "Men shall be lovers of their own selves, *covetous*—having a form of godliness but denying the power thereof. . . . . *Of this sort are they* which creep into houses, and lead captive silly women; . . . men of corrupt minds, reprobate concerning the faith." In the passage from which these sentences are taken, the Apostle begins by predicting the future corruption of the clerical order, which was to take place in an age subsequent to the Apostolic, but he glides, as you perceive, in the words quoted, into a reference to *a known and admitted matter of fact.* It was a fact that the corruption had already begun; and that there were *then* men, selfish and covetous, with a form of godliness but without the reality;—who, in the guise of Christian teachers, "crept into men's houses," got hold of the women, played upon their weaknesses, their morbid sensibility, their religious apprehensions, their mental unstableness and liking for something new, and thus by various arts securing such a spiritual ascendancy over them, that

they became as it were their "captives," and as such would do anything for them,—a result which was the object aimed at from the first, that it might be turned to account, and made the means of increasing their "base gain."

1 Tim. vi. 3. "These things teach and exhort. If any man teach otherwise, and consent not to wholesome words, even the words of our Lord Jesus Christ and to the doctrine which is according to godliness, he is proud, knowing nothing .... of corrupt mind and destitute of the truth, *supposing that gain is godliness,*"—or, rather that "godliness is gain,"—that the profession of it may be adopted, or its service assumed, simply with a view to a profitable pecuniary result!

In the 2nd Epistle of Peter, and the Epistle of Jude, there is a double description of a set of scoundrels who infested the Church, mingled in the social and sacred engagements of Christian fellowship, whose character is drawn in darker colours than we venture to reproduce. The most flagrant immoralities are attributed to them; every thing offensive in "the lusts" alike "of the flesh and of the mind." These, however, we shall not enumerate, but shall content ourselves with quoting so much of the description as serves to show that all these repulsive and loathsome phenomena were connected with COVETOUSNESS, *the root principle of all evil.* It is to be observed, then, that these men are represented as professing to be qualified to teach —they assumed to be "prophets," in the New Testament sense of being *preachers*. But they were "false prophets," bringing in "damnable heresies," and denying the Christian truth. "*With feigned words they made merchandise of the people.*" The flock was estimated according to the fleece. Living souls were thought of and talked about, as if they were made to be bought and sold and trafficked with for gain! Their "*hearts were exercised with covetous practices;*"—they had "forsaken the right way and had gone astray, following the way of Balaam,"—"who loved the wages of unrighteousness." They spake "great swelling words"—"boasted great things"—"promising liberty, while they themselves were the slaves of corruption." They found their account in all this for a time; but their "judgment" (or condemnation) lingered not, neither did the sentence of their perdition slumber. While they lived and rioted they were miserable and loathsome: and they were doomed of God to perish at last. "These are spots in your feasts of charity, feeding themselves without fear; clouds are they without water, carried about of winds; trees whose fruit withereth without fruit, twice dead, plucked up by the roots; raging waves of the sea foaming out their own shame; wandering stars, to whom is reserved the blackness of darkness for ever!"—a terrible picture that, of persons pretending to be Christian teachers, and who were looked up to and regarded as such, though the half of what is said of them has not been repeated.

With two references more, to illustrate matters of fact in the Apostolic age, we shall close this section of our argument. From the Epistle to the Philippians we gather what is not creditable to the purity and disinterestedness of the more prominent of the teachers at the church at Rome during the Apostles' imprisonment. In the first chapter, he speaks of some " who preached Christ of envy and strife ; of the spirit of contention, not sincerely," with a deliberate design to vex and annoy him, " supposing to add affliction to his bonds." Such conduct seems to us as strange as it is monstrous; but we get, I suppose, the key to it in the 2nd chapter, 19th verse. " I trust to send Timotheus shortly unto you : . . . . for *I have no man likeminded* who will naturally care for your state. *For all seek their own, not the things which are Jesus Christ's.*" " All seek their own:" a serious indictment that, especially as laid against ministers,—and such I take it to be from its connexion with the mention of Timothy. Paul needed the help and attendance of Timothy, and wishing to retain him might have proposed, therefore, to some resident officer of the Roman Church to undertake for him the journey to Philippi. There was not one of them who would do it! Not a soul would give up, for a short time, his personal interests, his comfort or convenience; or would incur the expense; or would run the risk of damaging his business, or in any way endanger his own concerns! Though they were, as we infer, the guides of the church, they had not learnt the lesson which the Apostle inculcates in this epistle—(2 c. v. 4) "Look not every man on his own things"—*his own personal interests or possessions*—"but every man also on the things of others. Let that mind be in you which was also in Christ Jesus."

What occurred on Paul's first imprisonment, occurred again on the occasion of the second, a few years afterwards. It was then attended with a still more lamentable instance of ministerial selfishness. In the 2nd Epistle to Timothy, the last letter Paul ever wrote—the latest at least that we have of his—when he was "such an one as Paul the aged," we find him recording that, "at his first answer, no man stood with him; but all forsook him;" and that one of his old enemies at Ephesus, Alexander the coppersmith, "had done him much evil;" he refers also to one and another of his friends and associates having been obliged to leave him at the call of duty; but the darkest stroke in the whole picture—that which reveals the saddest aspect in the desolateness to which he felt himself

abandoned—is contained in these words—"DEMAS
HATH FORSAKEN ME ; *having loved the present world,
and is departed into Thessalonica*."!*
On this statement you may remark, that Demas is
mentioned in the Epistle to Philemon, verse 24th,
as one of Paul's fellow-labourers, and is honourably
classed with Aristarchus, Epaphras, Mark, and
Luke. He is also mentioned in Colossians, iv. 14, in a
similar manner—" Luke the beloved Physician, and
Demas greet you." Both these epistles were written
during Paul's first imprisonment, so that Demas
appears to have stood by the Apostle, and to have
been a comfort to him, when he had to complain of
others, as we have seen, " who sought their own, not
the things that were Jesus Christ's." Now, however,
when things have got worse, and Paul has no hope
of liberation or life—when he is more in need therefore of solace and sympathy,—the courage of Demas
gives way, and his character utterly breaks down.—
" Demas hath *forsaken* me." The word is strong
and significant, implying complete, if not heartless
desertion. It is the word which occurs in the
subsequent verse, where he says that " no man stood
by him, but all forsook him." It is the word used
respecting the cowardly conduct of the disciples,
when Christ was seized by the soldiers,—" then all
the disciples forsook him and fled." It is the word

* II. Timothy iv. 10.

used to illustrate the constancy of the divine care by expressing what God did *not* do, thus presenting a contrast to the weakness of man :—" We are persecuted," says the Apostle, " but *not* forsaken ;" not abandoned or deserted by our Heavenly Friend. " Thou wilt not leave my soul in hell," or the place of the dead, says David, —spoken prospectively in the person of the Messiah ;—Thou wilt not forsake or abandon me there, but " wilt show me the path of life, and make me full of joy with thy countenance." " Demas hath forsaken me, *having loved the present world.*" There is here, perhaps, a designed contrast with the verse immediately preceding. In that Paul had expressed his persuasion that, having " fought the good fight," " finished his course," and " kept the faith," there was " laid up for him a crown of righteousness, which the Lord, the righteous judge, would give to him at the last day ;" and then he adds, and " not to me only, but unto all them also *that love his appearing.*" Immediately upon this he alludes to Demas as having deserted him ;— having run away from " the battle," given up " the race," and abandoned " the faith," because, instead of " loving" and looking for " the Lord's appearing," " he loved " and looked after " the present world." Something more seems to be implied than a momentary weakness,—that loss of nerve or sudden panic which may occasionally overcome even the brave and true. It would rather appear to have been a deliberate determination to abandon alike the Apostle and his Master for the sake of some secular advantage. He had to support himself, possibly, by some sort of business; and a good opening happening to present itself in Thessalonica, the opportunity of employment and the prospect of gain were too strong for him, especially when combined with the prospect of persecution if he remained at Rome;—so he set off, without saying a word to St. Paul, and forsook God to serve Mammon!

III.

In this way, then, the New Testament sets before us in positive and palpable facts belonging to the early church, the corrupting influence of the love of money, both in the ordinary members of the Christian community, and in the case of ministers and teachers;—some false, some true; some heretical, some orthodox; and one, at least, the friend and associate of the Apostles themselves. Passing from the facts of the first age, let us now look at some of the predictions of what was to come to pass in those that were to succeed, especially with respect to the covetousness and corruption which were to be developed in ministers, which, as we shall find, were to be attended with corresponding results in the people.

When Paul touched at Miletus, and sent to Ephesus for the elders of the Church, to address to them what he thought would be his last words, he thus spake to them after their arrival, "Take heed unto yourselves, and to all the flock, over which the Holy Ghost hath made you overseers, to feed the Church of God, which he hath purchased with his own blood. For I know this, that after my departure, shall *grievous wolves* enter in among you, *not sparing the flock*. Also of your own selves shall men arise, speaking perverse things, *to draw away disciples after them*."* There is here a distinct intimation of the ministry becoming, even in its highest offices, an instrument of rapacity; and that men would attach disciples to themselves to gratify at once their ambition and their covetousness.

In like manner, in both his first and second letter to Timothy, the Apostle, speaking of the evils that would appear in the Church, refers to the baseness, selfishness, and cupidity which should characterize those in the sacred office. " The Spirit speaketh expressly, that in the latter times some shall *depart from the faith*, giving heed to seducing spirits and doctrines of devils, *speaking lies in hypocrisy, having their consciences seared as with an hot iron*."† Men so described, whatever their rank or office in the Church, could only be animated

* Acts xx. 28—30. † I. Timothy iv. 1, 2.

by low motives; by the love of power, or the love of money; by one or more of the gross propensities which go to make up "the minding of earthly things" —"the lust of the flesh, the lust of the eye, and the pride of life." In the parallel passage, we have a full-length picture of these professed ministers of Christ, but who in reality are the servants of the devil;—a picture in which their inward corruption, beginning its manifestations with the outbreak of selfishness and cupidity, goes working on in every form of the flesh, till they are covered all over with "the swellings and excrescences of moral disease." "This know that *in the last days perilous times shall come. For men shall be lovers of their own selves, covetous*":—there is the root of the evil; then come the ramifications — "boasters, proud, blasphemers, disobedient to parents, unthankful, unholy, without natural affection — incontinent, fierce, despisers of them that are good, heady, high-minded, *lovers of pleasure more than lovers of God; having a form of godliness but denying the power thereof.*"* And that this description applies to persons in office,—to those we call ministers, ecclesiastics, or the clergy,—we showed before when referring to what immediately follows, that "*of this sort*" were they, who, in the guise of teachers, where then going about, leading

* II. Timothy iii. 1—7.

"captive" their dupes and disciples, professing to help them to "the knowledge of the truth;" but, in fact, "teaching things which they ought not for filthy lucre's sake."

The passages before referred to in the Epistle of Jude and the second of Peter, while descriptive of men who were then in the Church, are introduced by predictions of future degeneracy. "There were false prophets also among the people, *even as there shall be false teachers among you.* . . . . Many shall follow their pernicious ways . . . . and *through covetousness shall they with feigned words make merchandise of you*"—(II. Peter ii. 1—3.) "Murmurers, complainers," (complaining, I suppose, that they never got enough) they, "walking after their own lusts," will "have men's persons in admiration *because of advantage*"—(Jude v. 16.) All this was not to be without its effect upon the people, of whom it is said, in corresponding language, "The time will come when they will not endure sound doctrine; but after their own lusts shall they heap to themselves teachers having itching ears; and they shall turn away their ears from the truth, and shall be turned unto fables"—(II. Tim. iv. 3, 4.) So it was, and so it ever will be, "Like priest like people." The two classes mutually affect each other. A worldly priesthood will foster in the community the vices they give way to themselves. The ignorant masses will be willing to be corrupted. " The prophets prophesy falsely, and the priests rule by their means ; and my people love to have it so ; but what will ye do in the end thereof ? "

IV.

We have thus set before you this morning three things. First, certain recorded New Testament facts, showing the bad influence of the love of money on private Christians. Secondly, we have noticed other facts, similarly recorded, showing the same thing, the bad influence of the love of money on ministers and teachers. Thirdly, we have referred to the Apostolic predictions of the corruption and apostacy of the last times, and these we have seen are intimately connected with a sordid and mercenary spirit in the priesthood, which breaks out into many and diversified forms of evil. We regret to say, that something yet remains of the dark side of the subject. What it is, we must leave to be exhibited in a future discourse.

Sermon V.

LUKE xvi. 22, 23.

"The rich man died, and was buried; and in hell he lift up his eyes, being in torments."

YOU have seen so many proofs of our first proposition "that money may be a bad thing,"—it has been illustrated in so many ways, and by so large and varied a collection of facts,—that you may be disposed to think that nothing more, or nothing new, can be added. As we intimated, however, last Sunday, something does yet remain of the darker side of the subject we are discussing. Nothing, more, indeed, is to be adduced, or nothing worse, as to the bad influence of the love of money *here;* there are yet, however, to be noticed such glimpses as we get in the New Testament of its ultimate issues in a future world.

We may here notice, in a passing remark, a striking characteristic of the Gospel narrative, which you have no doubt often heard referred to. Of all biographies—in the Bible or in the world—that of our Lord is the most wonderful. In every respect it is full of interest.

There is nothing like studied artifice about it, and yet the gradual evolving of the story is marvellously conducted. The brief glances at the infancy of Jesus—the more minute record of his public life—his extraordinary works, his original conceptions, his popular parables, the tragic and touching circumstances that gather about his early death—all are wonderful. The wonderfulness, however, is to be seen, not so much in what is recorded of things done, and in what Christ as a teacher says, as in the absence of much that might have been looked for, and in what Christ does *not* say. If the subject had been put into the hands of a great human genius, one of your masters of fiction, —" GIVEN, the appearance in the flesh of the Son of God,—*write His life ;*" there can be no doubt that we should have had miracles springing up at every step. Nothing would have been natural. Infancy, boyhood, the school-house, the workshop (if these latter, indeed, had been thought of at all), would have been overlaid with the startling and the marvellous. In the imaginary discourses attributed to him there would have been the constant effort to fill them with revelations of the invisible world, as the proof that he had come from it, and was intimately familiar with and master of its mysteries. In the Gospels, however, there is a marked abstinence from all this. There are miracles, indeed, as might have been expected; but there are many vacant spaces in which none are to be seen, when the daily life of the august visitor resembles that of an ordinary man. There is no useless expenditure of supernatural power,—miracles are not done ostentatiously to evince it; they are never in themselves puerile or ridiculous, as is often the case in the apocryphal Gospels. As to the revelations of Jesus in respect to the unseen, there is really little, comparatively, of the sort. The wonder is that there is not more. What there is, is characterized by a sublime reticence. Nothing is said to gratify mere curiosity, or to excite wonder by prolonged and minute specification of particulars. And yet, when our Lord does touch on what belongs to the upper world and "His Father's house," what indications there are of his Divine knowledge!—of what he *could* have told us had he pleased! and with what serene and quiet composure he speaks of the unseen! His manner seems to show a personal familiarity with its sublime secrets; while *what* he says is spoken not for effect, but is simply adapted to stimulate spiritual thought and to leave upon the heart a moral impression.

In speaking of the condition of the lost, Jesus occasionally used strong expressions,—clothing spiritual ideas in figurative language. The most terrible of these were employed in denouncing sanctimonious hypocrisy, worn as a cover for the money-lust, when stigmatizing the Pharisees " who were covetous,"— " who devoured widows' houses, and for a pretence made long prayers." Once, he withdrew the curtain of the unseen world, that they might look into it for a moment. It was to exhibit the spectacle of *a rich man in hell.* Even in this picture, however, there is nothing like the elaborate minuteness which characterize the common representations of purgatory in catholic countries, or those in which Protestant preachers have sometimes indulged, when describing, in impassioned popular oratory, the condition of the damned!

In our subsequent remarks, we propose first to advert to what is naturally introduced by these introductory observations; and then to bring to a close this first part of our argument, by citing certain passages out of the Epistles, which will be seen to manifest advantage in the light of it.

With respect, then, to the ultimate issues in the future world of a spirit of worldliness, in the form of hoarding, selfishness, the love of money, we have four things; namely, two parables,—a fact,—and an Apostolic denunciation.

I.

The first parable was repeated at length in our second discourse, [page 39], and is usually denominated "the rich fool."* It was called forth by the request of one who wished Jesus to interfere in the settlement of a dispute about certain property to

* Luke xii. 16—21.

which he thought himself entitled. We have no reason to think that the man's claim was not well founded. Most likely it was. But he brought it before the wrong person, and urged it at a time and in a manner, which showed an utter insensibility to spiritual things, and the predominance of a low master passion. The parable would be the more pointed, in its bearings on his case, by the subject of it being understood to be one who had not acquired his property wrongfully. The claim of "the rich man" to what he possessed was undoubted. His wealth had come to him by God's blessing on his fields and vineyards. It was very great. The harvest had been so abundant, his land had brought forth so plentifully that he seemed at a loss to know what to do with the produce. In the thought of his heart, however, when he said "within himself" "what shall I do, because I have no room where to bestow my fruits?" there was more of the chuckle of inflated complacency, than of real perplexity as to what was to be done. At any rate, his only apprehension could be lest his crops should sustain injury by lying exposed, or being insecurely garnered; he had no thought of housing any of them in the stomachs of the starving or the pantries of the poor. He was ready with his design "to pull down his barns and build greater, and *there* to bestow *all* his fruits and his goods." A very proper procedure this, in one sense, under the circumstances;

but the utter selfishness with which it was associated in the mind of the speaker, is immediately made apparent by his letting out that he was thinking of nothing but his own enjoyment; secretly exulting, too, in the security and permanence of his possessions, as if he were lord over his own life! "I will say to my soul, Soul, thou hast much goods laid up for many years, take thine ease, eat, drink, and be merry." What an address for a man to make to his "soul"! What a poor, low, materialized idea of life is here indicated!—no thought of spiritual culture, moral effort, aspirations after usefulness, regard for others, sympathy with humanity, communion with heaven, *recognition*, even, of God! Nothing of the sort. And though, in the anticipated "eating and drinking and making merry," we have no right to suppose there was to be any degree of intemperance or excess, there was yet nothing but the selfish and sensual *in kind*, —connected with that boasting of the future, in his presuming on "many years," which is intolerable in one who "knows not what a day may bring forth."

"But," while the man thus "thought within himself," and resolved and reckoned after this fashion, God was looking down upon him from on high, and, seeing what was already at his door, though the poor wretch knew it not, *He* "said," within himself, " Fool " that thou art, "this night thy soul shall be required of thee; then whose shall those things be which thou hast provided?" Every word is emphatic, and every idea terrible. That "soul," which was to be indulged and pampered with material satisfactions, as if that was the end for which it was made, is to be delivered up, and an account given of what has been done with it. "This night *they shall require* thy soul." *He* was not aware of it, but at the very moment of exultant anticipation, "his soul was drawing nigh to the grave and his life to *the destroyers*." Those things he was storing for himself, were to pass into the hands of others. Of all he possessed he could take nothing away with him. "*So* is he,"—such a fool—" who layeth up treasure for himself, and is not rich towards God."

It is quite possible, you will remember, for a man to be rich in worldly possessions and rich also in divine endowments; but it is not possible to "lay up" for self *in an exclusive sense*, and "to lay up" for God too. It is possible (though difficult) to hold great wealth in such a way as not to presume upon it; —not to forget God,—not to employ it for mere selfish objects; to be ready too at any moment, or whenever required, to leave it without a sigh, so that, instead of death coming with a demand like an officer of justice, he may come as a divine messenger with an invitation to "the marriage supper of the Lamb." Thus a rich man, "rich in faith," instead of having his soul dragged out of him by the angels of judgment, may voluntarily breathe it forth into the hands of his Lord, "willing to depart," ready to be translated! But it was not thus with the rich man before us. It cannot be thus with those "that trust in their wealth and boast themselves in the multitude of their riches; whose inward thought is, that their houses shall continue for ever, their dwelling-places to all generations." While the man lived, "he blessed his soul;" when called away, "he died as the fool dieth." In the description of the event, the curtain falls just as it seems to be beginning to rise. The closing silence of the parable is eloquent. Nothing is said of the ultimate doom of this wealthy proprietor; no particulars are furnished, no picture attempted to be drawn. We hear of the midnight summons, and the sudden departure; the fact is stated, and that is all; its issues are *suggested*,—they are left for the reason and the conscience to conjecture.

II.

The second parable is the one to which we have already alluded, that of "the rich man and Lazarus."*
The condition of the dead is here set forth more distinctly, and with some appalling particulars. This, however, is not done merely to depict suffering, but to produce and intensify moral impression. Those who reject the authority of the Gospels, and feel

* Luke xvi. 19—31.

at liberty to dispute the teaching of Jesus, object to this parable that its obvious tendency, if not positively bad, is at least questionable. They fix upon the words of Abraham,—"Son, remember that thou in thy lifetime receivedst thy good things, and likewise Lazarus evil things; but now he is comforted, and thou art tormented." They then say, that this is nothing but a vulgar mode of flattering the poor at the expense of the rich. That the future condition of men is here represented as the result exclusively of external circumstances. Character has nothing to do with it. Just because here one man is rich and another poor, the tables are to be turned hereafter,— the poor to be solaced in Abraham's bosom, the rich tormented in burning flame! Very comforting, but very perilous, teaching for the poor.

Now, such an impression, however at first sight it may appear to be sustained by the words quoted, totally disappears when the parable is fairly interpreted as a whole. It is then seen that *character* is kept in view in every particular, and the moral teaching of the piece is justified.

In the first place, not only the uniform object of Christ's teaching, but the connection of this parable with what goes before, creates a *presumption*, at least, that he must have had his mind fixed upon something moral in the case both of the rich man and the poor. The chapter begins with the parable of the unjust steward, in which Christ sets forth the possibility of *so* using the resources of wealth, as to make it productive of good issues hereafter. He insists on the importance of fidelity in this matter; shewing, that while that would be indicative of universal conscientiousness, unfaithfulness would imply the neglect of spiritual culture and the forgetfulness of divine duties. His words, highly figurative as they are, are but another form of the saying, "he that loves God will love his brother also; he that loves not his brother loves not God." Following this up with a warning against the love and service of Mammon, he is derided by the Pharisees whose covetousness led them to ridicule such lessons. Glancing at their perversion of the teaching of Moses as accounting for their blindness in relation to his own, he proceeds to introduce the parable before us, obviously with the express and special intention of illustrating *not* the evil of merely *having* money, but *one mode of unfaithfulness in the use of it*. Here again the point of the parable is to be seen in the rich man being free from degrading crime or vice. He is not unjust, fraudulent, impure, —making money by wrong and spending it in riot. He may be supposed to be unstained in his personal habits, upright in his dealings, worthy as a citizen, easy, good-natured, bland, courteous. With all this, however, he is utterly selfish, and lives only for his own enjoyment. He can afford anything; has command over all material satisfactions; and so "he fares sumptuously every day," has his "fine linen" as a customary indulgence, and his robe of "purple" for great occasions. The beggar at his door would be thankful for "the crumbs that fall from his table;" but if ever he gets them, he owes it more to the compassion of the servants than the thoughtfulness of the master. This man, then, has large wealth, but he "makes no friends" by kindness in the use of it. His possessions are a "stewardship," —but he is not faithful to Him to whom he is accountable. Insensibility to or neglect of one set of duties, implies the violation or forgetfulness of others. The whole description is that of a thoroughly worldly and godless man; respectable, we admit, in the estimation of society, but without faith in anything higher than in what he can employ "to make himself comfortable." He lives a life of refined and tolerated luxury, has no thought of claims on him from without, and no idea of a final reckoning.—" May he not do what he likes with his own!" Now in all this there is a moral element, and all this is clearly involved in the significance of the parable. "Dives," as we call him, is not weighed and measured simply by what he *has*,—the accident of wealth; but by what he *is*,—the state of the heart, his habits and conduct in relation at once to man and God.

It is fair, I say, to presume that our Lord *meant* to

suggest to his incredulous auditors these moral ideas in drawing the picture of the rich man. This presumption expands into *probability*, when we connect with himself what the man says about his brothers. His words convey the impression that they were living careless and godless lives; without thought of, and without preparation for the inevitable future. They needed to "repent,"—to become altered in character; and in order to this, they needed to be "persuaded" of the reality and importance of spiritual things. They were either Sadducees, disbelieving the truth, or they were men of the world, disregarding the power of it. Now, it is not necessary to suppose him to have been worse than his brothers, but it is reasonable to infer that he was very much like them. His consciousness seems to be, that he had lived as they were living;— without a sense of personal responsibility, without faithfulness to the stewardship with which God had entrusted him—the thoughtful and conscientious management of wealth. The light reflected from the implied character of the members of his family, thus increases our conviction respecting his own.

But that Christ meant to fix attention on moral character, and not merely on external circumstances, becomes *certain*, when we rightly reflect on another thing. In the region of repose and blessedness, which forms the other division of the unseen state—

(according to the then prevalent popular notions, which our Lord adopts for the purpose of instruction);—in this region, he places one who, when he was upon earth, was "very rich;" rich in all sorts of substance,—in flocks and herds, camels and asses, silver and gold;—a man far richer, we may presume, than the "Dives" of the parable! Hence, the proof is complete, and the conclusion certain, that our Lord here teaches *not* merely that the poor are to be "comforted" and the rich "tormented" in the next world, *simply as such,* and without respect to higher considerations. If so, Abraham could not have been appropriately placed where we find him. The true lesson comes out with irresistible force by this last touch. Yes, Abraham was rich, very rich, wealthy among the opulent; but riches were not *his* "good things," nor anything they could command or purchase. He did not live for them, confide in them, or waste them on himself. He walked "by faith," communed with God, felt the reality of spiritual objects, regarded the world as not his rest, sought "another country, even an heavenly," believed in, and looked for *that.* It was the rich man's want of Abraham's resolute religious faith, not his riches, which consigned him to condemnation. Had he been in harmony with Abraham in respect to character, he would, doubtless, have found himself in safety at his side. It is obvious to remark, that the same principle applies to Lazarus. His mere poverty was no virtue. In themselves, his rags and sores were not the ground of his being permitted to share the blessedness of the Patriarch. His being placed where we find him, is intended to indicate that he was a partaker of Abraham's faith; as such, and only as such, could he be "a fellow heir with him" of his glorious rest.

The parable, then, justly interpreted, not only is not open to the infidel objection, but is fraught with the most solemn and appropriate lessons to rich men. Its bearing, indeed, is not only on the absolutely opulent, but on all who have the means of enjoying life; who are free from anxiety; who are able to command the comforts and elegancies belonging to their station. Without being rich, it is quite possible to copy the selfishness of the rich man. You do this, if you provide only for your daily satisfactions; enjoying you own "fulness of bread" with no sense of pecuniary stewardship, no reference to Him who requires that expenditure should have other objects besides what are personal, and should include the exercise of a regulated liberality and a thoughtful beneficence. The rich man had no feeling of animosity towards Lazarus; only, *he did not think of him.* He might even have given to such cases, *if asked;* but he did not *"consider* the poor," nor think of *" devising* liberal things." He had no notion of living for anything, here or hereafter, by the *conscientious* employment of what he possessed. The consequence was, that the discovery of his obligation to do so came when it could not be fulfilled. Hell itself may consist in this—it will certainly be aggravated by it—the discovery and apprehension of truth and duty *too late*. Let all, then, remember, that while the parable especially concerns rich men, yet it is not necessary to have great wealth for the sin of Dives to be committed,— just as it is not necessary to gain " the *whole* world " in order to " lose the soul."

Sermon VI.

Acts I. 25.

. . . "This ministry and apostleship, from which Judas by transgression fell, *that he might go to his own place.*"

IT was intimated last Sunday that, in respect to the ultimate issues in a future world of the love of money, we have in the New Testament four things, namely, two parables—a fact—and an apostolic denunciation. The two parables—The rich fool, and the rich man and Lazarus—have been noticed. The two remaining things have now to be considered.

The *fact* referred to is the case of Judas. This man is never mentioned in the enumeration of the names of the Apostles, without a brand being stamped upon his :—"Judas, *who was the traitor ;*"—"Judas Iscariot, *who also betrayed him.*" An indelible stigma has thus always attached to him. It has been thought, however, that his conduct may admit of an explanation, which would mitigate the popular impression of his guilt. It may be supposed, it is said, that he was not actuated by the love of money; that he never contemplated injury to Jesus;—that he was only weary of our Lord's delay in declaring himself, and setting up his kingdom; that he wished *to force* him to do this; and, therefore, determined to bring him into circumstances that would oblige him to act. For this purpose he planned to put him into the hands of his enemies—never dreaming that he would allow himself to be condemned; believing, rather, that he would exert his power upon *them*, " subdue the people under him;" and ascend " the throne of his father David." Instead, therefore, of his imagining that he was committing a crime, for which his name and memory might be reprobated, it is to be supposed that, in his own estimation, he was only contemplating a stroke of policy;—one, too, the results of which would be such as to entitle him to the lasting gratitude of his colleagues, and which even Jesus himself might, when accomplished, recognize and reward by according to him in " The kingdom" one of its highest positions. The theory is ingenious; it offers relief; one could almost wish it to be true. But it attributes, we fear, to "the traitor" attributes of mind which hardly belonged to him; and it does not seem consistent with the plain meaning of the words of the narrative, or with the whole of the recorded facts of the case. We shall not, however, discuss the question, but shall just give our own view of the character of Judas, and show the bearing of his conduct on the illustration of what we have in hand.

I.

In spite of the mystery attaching to the subject from the ultimate act of the man being "from the beginning" known to Jesus, and from its being spoken of as fulfilling that "that was written of him."—(a mystery, by the way, which attaches to every human action, considered as the object of Divine foreknowledge, men, all the time, feeling within them the consciousness of freedom and the sense of responsibility, and that probation is a reality and not a make-believe)—in spite of this, we feel warranted to look at Judas exactly as we look at any other man. To us, he was made up of the same elements that go to constitute ordinary humanity, and had to go through, in principle, the same sort of trial. He had to be exposed to temptation, but was capable of resistance; he was liable to err, to falter, to fall, but there was provided for him adequate and opportune help. From peculiarity of temperament, or the influence of circumstances, he might, like many of us, have been impelled or drawn towards certain sins, but he was not therefore necessitated to commit them. He came in contact with influences which might have been beneficial, which were intended to fortify him against himself, and to develope and give the victory to the good and the better which might be struggling within him against their opposites. We refuse to regard the case of Judas as exceptional. We look at him and judge him as we look at and judge any one else of whose ultimate condition, as to character and destiny, we know nothing, though it may be distinctly and certainly known to God.

Judas, then, we may suppose, like the other apostles, or some of them, might have been first acted upon by the preaching of John the Baptist. It is quite possible that he might have been impressed by his words of warning and his call to repentance. But however that might be, he certainly became a disciple of Jesus. As such, he must have been distinguished by constancy of attendance, propriety of behaviour, and other apparently good qualities, for him to have been chosen to the apostleship—the choice, as we presume, having had nothing about it to shock observers, though we, of course, knowing what we do, may deem it strange;—strange, that Jesus should have placed near himself, and put into office, one whom he knew was ultimately to betray him! There was probably a lesson for all time in the fact that such a man was put into the ministry; but into that we need not enter. As to his being chosen, under the circumstances, it is to be remembered, that Christ's knowledge of the result which would issue after trial, was no more an obstacle to his submitting Judas to it, or placing him under influences, which, if yielded to, would be his salvation—than God's knowledge of the end is an obstacle to *His* acting in this way towards each of us. The mere intellect cannot penetrate the mystery, or sound its depths, but the mind must acquiesce in the fact; for while the idea of God suggests to the reason His attribute of omniscience, experience and consciousness assure us of our own moral probation. We feel that that is a reality, and that the Divine wish, so to speak, is sincere, "that men would listen to Him and live," even when He knows that they will refuse and perish. "And Elisha said, go, say unto him *thou mayest certainly recover:* howbeit the Lord hath showed me that *he shall surely die.* And the man of God wept."

Judas was numbered with the twelve. He was called to high service, the thought of which, had his nature been ingenuous, might have raised what was low in him and purified what was corrupt; and he was habitually under the influence of a Teacher whose life and lessons, example and discourse, might have checked his native impulses to evil, and have delivered him from "the snare of the Devil" by whatever lust he was seeking to enthral him. We have no right to say that deep impressions were never made upon him, or that there was not at times a conscious struggle in his mind between the worser and the better, good and evil, duty and temptation. It might be after strong contest that the mean and base got the better of him, and his sordid propensities achieved a triumph. He became the treasurer of the apostolic company. With his probable peculiarity of temperament, and natural tendency to covetousness, this, to him, was a source of temptation. Jesus, it may be thought, might have saved him from this danger by preventing the appointment; but it was not his way, as it is not God's to save character by preventing temptation: it is rather through that, that character is at once to be tested and improved. In the case of Judas, temptation prevailed. He yielded to it and sinned. The first act ripened into a habit, and the habit became inveterate and deadly. "Lust when it hath conceived bringeth forth sin, and sin being matured bringeth forth death." What Judas became, in the office he held, is expressly stated. He robbed the bank—small as the amount in it must ever have been. He did not do this at a stroke,—absconding with what he was entrusted with at some period when the purse might have been unusually full. He pilfered. Every now and then he secreted small sums. " He had the bag," and had power over it, and " he stole what was put therein," for " he was a thief." Even though it may be said that the word rendered "stole" need not mean more than that he had the money in his custody, very little is gained for Judas by that. The positive, unequivocal record remains, "*he was a thief.*" Even if that should refer to his general character, as one ready to steal from anybody, or in the habit of doing it, still it would imply, standing where it does, that he put his hand into the purse he bore.

II.

Now, only think of the complicated sin into which the love of money, when permitted to rule as a governing lust, led this man. It would be giving Judas credit for a more far-seeing faculty than any we can attribute to him, to suppose that from the first he calculated on opportunities, in consequence of his becoming a disciple of Jesus, of indulging his sordid propensities and accumulating base gain. He could not know he was to be called to the apostleship; he could not foresee that there would be a common purse; he could not count on being entrusted with it,—or be supposed to have planned that there should be such a purse, and to get it into his power, and to make something out of that. He might indeed have had the lowest possible thoughts of Christ's kingdom, and have admitted his pretensions and joined himself to him from the meanest of motives. Even with this, however, when Christ forbad his representatives to take with them purse, money, or scrip when doing his work, an influence was brought to bear on them by which even Judas might have been affected, and so have caught the idea of a life of faith. But subsequent circumstances, already adverted to, awoke into activity his bad nature, and, that becoming dominant, he went on adding sin to sin and villany to villany. Out of what he was entrusted with he had sometimes to buy food, occasionally, perhaps, to pay for lodgings; now to provide for a passover, now to give to the poor,—and he so managed as to make a purse for himself by little peculations. You cannot but see that a number of different forms of sin would be necessary to insure success. There would often be verbal falsehood;—he had spent so much on such an occasion, given so much on another, when he had in each case parted with less, putting the difference in his pocket. He had to falsify his accounts. For a certain article he had given five pieces of silver; he "took his bill," and "put down" eight. Then the systematic hypocrisy of the man!—all the time he was doing this, he was keeping up appearances as a disciple and an apostle,—very likely simulating more than usual zeal, preaching and praying with enforced fervour to prevent suspicion. The contemptible meanness, the cruelty, too, of abstracting from the little store of those who never had much, and whose dependence, for the most part, was on the charitable "ministrations" of those who were not rich! But what at once aggravates his sin, and shows its terrible effect on his moral nature, is this, that all the time he was secretly indulging his sordid greed, and availing himself of every opportunity to obey it, he was an auditor and associate of Jesus,—heard his words, and saw his life. In his ears were delivered the sermon on the mount—the warnings against laying up treasure on earth—the assertion of the impossibility of serving God and Mammon—the rebuke of the man whose heart was in his "inheritance"—the denunciation of covetousness—the sorrowful exclamation extorted by the conduct of the young ruler,—the comparison between a rich man getting into heaven and a camel going through the eye of a needle—the parable of the wealthy proprietor, of the unjust steward, of the rich man and Lazarus; —all these, the probability is, Judas heard;—in addition to which, there were the discourses expository of spiritual truth,—the high thoughts so adapted to loosen the soul from earth and to lift it to heaven— "the words of eternal life;"—and there were the prayers of Jesus, and his private intercourse, his conversations in "the garden," whither "he often resorted with his disciples;"—Judas "knew the place,"—it ought to have been filled to him with the most sacred and subduing memories;—but in spite of everything he heard, saw, felt, he went on coveting, purloining, lying, till his whole nature was filled with the devil and he was capable of anything. Unless he himself had set open the door of his heart for Satan to enter, he could not have entered, or could not have "filled it,"—for even the great Tempter can only tempt. Judas gave himself up to the worst influences. He could see nothing but through the medium of covetousness; purpose nothing but as prompted by its power. When Mary broke the box of ointment, pouring out on the head of Jesus the expression at once of her love and sorrow, Judas could see in it nothing but "waste." He could deliberately plan the Lord's betrayal, — go to the priests,—make his bargain,—return in time to be unsuspected,—and, when returned, could take his customary place among the twelve, and seem as faithful and true as the rest! He suffered Jesus to wash his feet, and to treat him as one of his "friends," a few hours only before his crime was arranged to be accomplished. He kept up appearances to the last. Even when he guided the armed multitude to seize forcibly the person of Jesus he advanced with the appearance of friendship, having previously agreed that the sign of recognition should be the token of love! He did his work and he had his reward. He "sold the innocent blood," and grasped "the wages of unrighteousness." That he was filled with remorse when he saw that Jesus was condemned, is no proof that he had not contemplated that. Many a deliberately-planned murder has, when accomplished, caused a revulsion of feeling in the murderer, and made him wish that he had not done it. It was thus with Judas. The deed being done,—it, himself, Jesus, the work, the reward, the past, the future, everything appeared in a new light;—a fearful, lurid light. He tried to undo the evil when too late. Instead of sympathy or aid, he received from the priests coldness and scorn. His soul was in flames; and the pieces of silver seemed in his hands to have become coals of fire. He flung them from him,—threw them away,—that Money he had so much loved, for which he had sighed, plotted and sinned;—it was an object of aversion and abhorrence now. The "unrighteous Mammon," true to his character, had proved "deceitful." By false promises he had lured Judas to his ruin, and then abandoned him. What he had served as a God turned out a Demon;—one that flattered to betray, and which, when successful, despised his victim and laughed at his folly. Stung and exasperated, loathing life, driven to despair, the wretched man "went and hanged himself." From "his ministry and apostleship, Judas, by transgression, fell, that he might go to his own place."

"*That he might go to his own place.*" It need not be concealed that there are those who regard these words as not spoken of Judas, but of him, whomsoever he might prove to be, who should be chosen to succeed him. The sense of the passage, on this hypothesis, might be put thus :—The apostles wishing to fill up, by lot, the vacancy that had occurred in their number, appointed two, and then prayed to God, asking Him to show "which of the two He had chosen," that, *being* chosen, "he might go to his own place,"—take his proper position—"his part,' with the twelve, "in that ministry and apostleship, from which Judas by transgression fell." The suggestion is, at least, ingenious. We will not assert that it may not be accepted instead of what is popularly understood by the words. Nevertheless, we think that the idea which our translation conveys to the common mind is more likely to be correct, and to be more in accordance with what Peter meant, than any other. *His own place!*—that for which alone he was morally fit. As we read of being made "*meet* for the inheritance of the saints in light ;" and of " vessels of wrath *fitted* for destruction ;" so we have here, as we imagine, the idea of one who had so " fallen by his iniquity," that his *own proper place*, in God's universe, could only be found in " the outer darkness,"— among devils and damned souls ! And this was the result of the love of money !

Terrible words these. They are authorized, however, by Jesus himself, for it was *He* who spake of those who, not believing, should be "damned," and who described the "cursed" and the lost as departing into the fire "prepared for the Devil and his angels." Of course *his* words were always intended to mean something, and those thus referred to must have been intended to mean something terrible. Even on such authority, however, we dread to repeat them, and would rather not do it, were it not imperative to do so from fidelity to truth—the truth belonging to the subject which we have on hand. That we speak under such a necessity will be seen by the last thing which has here to be noticed,—namely, that apostolic denunciation with the quotation of which the first part of our general argument is about to be concluded.

III.

We refer to the words of St. James, chapter v. verse 1, "*Go to now, ye rich men, weep and howl for your miseries that shall come upon you. Your riches are corrupted, and your garments are moth-eaten. Your gold and silver is cankered! and the rust of them shall be a witness against you, and shall eat your flesh as it were fire. Ye have heaped treasure together for the last days.*" No paraphrase or expansion of this statement, however copious or eloquent, could add to the force and pungency of the words themselves, as simply read or heard without note or comment. It is true that the "rich men" here denounced are regarded as immoral and unjust, sensual and fraudulent; "the hire of the labourers who have reaped down their fields," is "kept back;" "the cries of the defrauded have entered into the ears of the Lord of Sabaoth;" they have "lived in pleasure and been wanton," and in their wantonness "have killed" the unresisting and the just. We do not, of course, bring such a railing accusation against rich men—men simply regarded as rich—as to attribute to them any such sins. Still, we do say that the words have a fearful aspect towards those who are the possessors of large wealth, *if they are unfaithful to their trust*, selfish and covetous. For, just as the divine gift of manna, if hoarded and kept unused, bred worms, and stank, and putrified—so, God's great gift of money, which might be put, and was intended to be put, to high service, if not used, but kept back, heaped up, shut away from air and sunlight, will become corroded and cankered, useless as a moth-eaten garment, and will contract rust,—rust which shall not only mar and destroy it, eating into it till it becomes to its possessor an utterly worthless thing, but which shall witness against him before God, testifying to the fact of his unfaithfulness —itself being the visible and palpable proof thereof —and shall thus eat into his flesh as it were fire;

eat into his whole nature, here and hereafter—first burning and drying it up by a tormenting sin, and then consuming it by an accordant but worser punishment. Gold, not only ill-gotten gold, but that which is simply unused, kept back from God's service and man's need, will turn at last into so much pitch and bitumen, and burst into flame round its miserable owner! He will then find out that, in increasing and "heaping up treasure for himself," he was only "*treasuring up wrath against the day of wrath and the revelation of the righteous judgment of God.*"

But we drop the curtain over these awful intimations of *the future*, and would rather leave them to your own thoughts, than attempt to deepen or aggravate their impression by words of ours.

CONCLUDING SECTION

TO

PART FIRST.

"*Money may be a bad thing*, but it may be put to a very good use." Such were the two aspects of the subject, which it seemed to present to us as we approached it. The first or dark side, has now been fully examined and exhibited. You have seen how the love of money obstructs the entrance of light into the soul, and hinders a man's acceptance of the kingdom of God; how it provokes opposition to the truth, and resists the drawings and monitions of the spirit; how it struggles against the beginnings of religion, and cripples and corrupts it at every stage ; how it debases the ministry, demoralizes the people, saps principle, destroys character, inflames lust, breeds error, prompts to meanness, falsehood, hypocrisy, tarnishes reputation, disturbs the Church, insults God ! And how, after bringing forth these and other evils—evils more numerous than we can recount, and more malignant and bitter than we can describe—it finishes its course and perfects its work by consigning its victims to such society as "the rich man who died and was buried, and who, in hell, lifted up his eyes, being in torments."

Leaving, however, now, this side of the subject, as it has been set forth before you, we shall conclude this first part of our argument by quoting and arranging, in a sort of rude order, various apostolic statements respecting Covetousness, which will be seen we think to advantage by being looked at in the light of what has been thus far said. Remembering what has been proved, by Scripture testimony, as to that money-lust which is " the root of all evil," you will not wonder at the way you will find it spoken of, or at the place it occupies, in the arguments, admonitions, and general teaching of St. Paul; nor will you be surprised to find that he was scrupulously careful to avoid whatever might, by the remotest possibility, give rise to any suspicion against himself, or have the appearance of his being tainted by that which he condemned.

Without comment or remark, then, or very little of either,—we request you to note the following things :—

I.

First. COVETOUSNESS *is enumerated among the proofs of the apostacy and as illustrative of the extreme wickedness of the Gentiles.* Romans i. 28—32. " And even as they did not like to retain God in their knowledge, God gave them over to a reprobate mind, to do those things which are not convenient; being filled with all unrighteousnes, fornication, wickedness, COVETOUSNESS, maliciousness; full of envy, murder, debate, deceit, malignity; whisperers, backbiters, haters of God, despiteful, proud, boasters, inventors of evil things, disobedient to parents, without understanding, covenant-breakers, without natural affection, implacable, unmerciful: who knowing the judgment of God, that they which commit such things are worthy of death, not only do the same, but have pleasure in them that do them."

Second. COVETOUSNESS *is reckoned among the works of the flesh, and is associated with the worst sins against which Christians can be warned.* 1 Cor: vi. 9. 10. " Know ye not that the unrighteous shall not inherit the kingdom of God? Be not deceived: neither fornicators, nor idolaters, nor adulterers, nor effeminate, nor abusers of themselves with mankind, nor thieves, nor COVETOUS, nor drunkards, nor revilers, nor extortioners, shall inherit the kingdom of God."

Third. COVETOUSNESS *is stigmatized as idolatry, and is classed with those outbreaks of evil on account of which God's wrath is threatened against the workers of iniquity.* Eph: v. 1. 3. Col: iii. 5. " Be followers of God as dear children . . . . But fornication, and all uncleanness, or COVETOUSNESS, let it not be once named among you, as becometh saints . . . . For this ye know, that no whoremonger, nor unclean person, nor COVETOUS *man, who is an idolater*, hath any inheritance in the kingdom of Christ and of God." " Mortify your members which are upon the earth; fornication, uncleanness, inordinate affection, evil concupiscence, and COVETOUSNESS, *which is idolatry:* for which things' sake the wrath of God cometh on the children of disobedience."

Fourth. COVETOUSNESS *is made the ground of refusing, to one professing to be a Christian, that Christian recognition which would acknowledge him as a brother.* 1 Cor. v.

9—11. "I wrote unto you in an epistle not to company with fornicators; yet not altogether with the fornicators of this world, or with *the covetous*, or with extortioners, or with idolaters; for then must ye needs go out of the world. But now I have written unto you not to keep company, *if any man that is called a brother* be a fornicator, or COVETOUS, *with such an one no not to eat.*"

These are remarkable sayings, and ought to have weight with Christians everywhere and always. Especially perhaps ought they to be pondered in an age and country distinguished by commercial activity, feverish competition, and large success; where, too, fortunes are *saved* as well as *made*,— gathered by habits which may begin in necessity, but which, becoming fixed and inveterate, change from prudential carefulness to covetous greed—from the allowable desire of money as an instrument, to the unhallowed and hardening love of it as an end. It is often sad to see, in many who begin religiously, the changes that will be produced, by rise in life, accumulation of property, altered position,—sometimes in the form of display and expenditure, which encroaches on the zeal and liberality of former years, when they could give more though in the receipt of less; sometimes in that tightening of the hand which results from their neglect of the Divine admonition, "when riches increase *set not your heart upon them.*" In the passages just quoted, you cannot but notice the very bad company in which covetousness is always found. Its friends and associates, so to speak, are the blackest of the vices; and though by such enumeration it is not intended to be said that they are always, or even often, to be *seen* together, yet it is meant that there is a family connexion amongst them, as springing from a common vitiated ancestry. It may be observed, too, that the foregoing statements commence by placing covetousness among the things which were aggravated by the separation of the old Gentile world from the original primitive Church of God; and they conclude by putting it among those things, *which would justify the separation of a professed Christian man from the companionship and communion of God's Church now.* Rather startling doctrine that, for those overladen, rich, niggardly churls, who are to be found in all ecclesiastical organizations,—covetousness being about the only great damning vice which can be indulged and clung to in connexion with a recognized modern religious profession!

II.

Again. As the general argument prepared you to hear without surprise the several statements which have just been quoted, so these statements will be an appropriate introduction to another class of passages which are to be found in the apostolic letters.

We refer to *such as demand a perfect freedom from the love of money in those who sustain office in the church.* These are to be found in what are called the Pastoral Epistles, and in the first Epistle of Peter.

1 Tim : iii. 1. "This is a true saying. If a man desire the office of a bishop, he desireth a good work. *A bishop* then must be blameless .... of good behaviour, given to hospitality, apt to teach .... *not greedy of filthy lucre* .... not *covetous* .... Moreover, he must have a good report of them that are without."

"Likewise must *the Deacons* be grave, not double-tongued, not given to much wine, *not greedy of filthy lucre:* holding the mystery of the faith in a pure conscience."

1 Tim : vi. 3. "If any man consent not to wholesome words even the words of our Lord Jesus, and to the doctrine which is according to godliness; he is proud, knowing nothing .... destitute of the truth, *supposing that gain is godliness.* FROM SUCH WITHDRAW THYSELF. But godliness with contentment is great gain. For we brought nothing into this world, and it is certain we can carry nothing out. And having food and raiment let us therewith be content. *But they th t will be rich fall into temptation and a snare;* .... *For the love of money is the root of all evil:* .... BUT THOU, O MAN OF GOD, FLEE THESE THINGS; and follow after righteousness, godliness, faith, love, patience, meekness. .... I give thee charge, in the sight of God .... and before Christ Jesus .... that thou keep this commandment without spot, unrebukable, until the appearing of our Lord Jesus Christ."

Titus i. 7. "*A bishop* must be blameless, as the steward of God; .... *not given to filthy lucre;* but a lover of hospitality, a lover of good men .... holding fast the faithful word as he hath been taught, *that he may be able by sound doctrine* both to exhort and to convince the gainsayers. For there are many unruly and *vain talkers and deceivers :* .... whose mouths must be stopped, who subvert whole houses, *teaching things which they ought not, for filthy lucre's sake."*

1 Peter v. 1. " *The elders* which are among you I exhort, who am also an elder; .... feed the flock of God which is among you, taking the oversight thereof, not by constraint but willingly; *not for filthy lucre*, but of a ready mind; .... and when the chief shepherd shall appear, ye shall receive a crown of glory that fadeth not away."

These passages require no comment. They may be left to make their own impression. It may be remarked, however, that the solicitude they evince, on the part of the Apostles, for the unsullied purity of the sacred office, for an exemplary freedom from sordid motives in those invested with the ministerial character, may prepare us for another class of passages, in which the same men *disclaim for themselves* all selfish and unworthy aims, and appeal to their known acts, their habitual behaviour, in proof and vindication of their boast. Weigh the following :—

III.

1 Thess; ii. 5. "Our exhortation was not of deceit, nor of uncleanness, nor in guile : but as we were allowed of God to be put in trust of the Gospel, even so we speak; not as pleasing men, but God which trieth our hearts.

APOSTOLIC EXAMPLE. 135

For neither at any time used we flattering words, as ye know, nor *a cloak of covetousness;* GOD IS WITNESS: nor of men sought we glory, neither of you, nor yet of others, *when we might have been burdensome, as the apostles of Christ.* But we were gentle among you, even as a nurse cherisheth her children : so being affectionately desirous of you, we were willing to have imparted unto you not the Gospel of God only, but also our own souls, because ye were dear unto us. *For ye remember, brethren, our labour and travail;* for *labouring night and day, because we would not be chargeable unto any of you,* we preached unto you the Gospel of God. *Ye are witnesses, and God also,* how holily and justly and unblameably we behaved ourselves among you that believe."

2 Cor. xi. 7. " Have I committed an offence. . . . . . *because I have preached unto you the Gospel of God freely?* I robbed other churches, taking wages of them, to do you service. And when I was present with you, *and wanted,* I was *chargeable to no man;* for that which was lacking to me the brethren which came from Macedonia supplied: and *in all things I have kept myself from being burdensome unto you, and so will I keep myself.* As the truth of Christ is in me, no man shall stop me of this boasting in the region of Achaia. Wherefore? because I love you not? God knoweth. But what I do, that I will do, *that I may cut off occasion from them that desire occasion.*"

xii. 13. "What is it wherein ye were inferior to other churches, except it be that I myself was not burdensome to you? *Forgive me this wrong.* Behold, the third time I am ready to come to you; and *I will not be burdensome to you:* for I SEEK NOT YOURS BUT YOU. . . . . But be it so, I did not burden you; nevertheless, being crafty, (they say,) I caught you with guile. *Did I make a gain of you by any of them whom I sent unto you?* I desired Titus, and with him I sent a brother. *Did Titus make a gain of you? Walked we not in the same spirit? Walked we not in the same steps?*

Looking at these passages in the light of our general argument, they stand out with remarkable distinctness, and wonderfully illustrate the apostolic character. Though they are taken from the writings of St. Paul, we regard them as uttered in the name of his colleagues as well as himself, and that they represent, therefore, what was common to them all.

Thus it was, then, that the apostles exemplified in themselves the purity of motive, simplicity of purpose, high aims, noble superiority to worldly influences, and every other form of disinterested virtue, which they required of those who were to be permitted to rule or minister in the Church. On proper occasions they could assert their own right to a pecuniary return, and insist that others "who did well" should be deemed worthy of fitting recompense.[*] They were not forbidden to receive support, in the form of "carnal things," from those to whom they imparted spiritual things. There was nothing in this, considered in itself, but a simple and natural "sowing" and "reaping." It was in harmony with the spirit of the former economy; it was the law of Christ "that they that preached the Gospel should live of the Gospel." Paul had not only power, if he

---

[*] 1 Tim. v. 17, 18.

chose to exercise it, to "forbear working"—to give up providing for himself by his own labour,—but to draw on the churches for a wife's support as well as his own, should he so will.* St. Peter's injunction " to take the oversight " of the flock, "*not* for filthy lucre," implies the existence of such pecuniary arrangements as might make it possible for such a motive to come into play. But with all this, Paul at least—if some others did not—waived his right, sunk his claim, and chose to depend on his own manual labour, working at night, to earn money for his needs and for those that were with him, that he might so preach and minister during the day, as "not to hinder the Gospel of Christ."

IV.

But it may be well to notice some passages of a different import, illustrative of other points in the apostolic character. Observe the following:—

a.

Philip: iv. 10. " I rejoice in the Lord greatly, that now at the last your care of me hath flourished again; wherein ye were also careful, but ye lacked opportunity. *Not that I speak in respect of want; for I have learned, in whatever state I am, therewith to be content.* . . . . Notwithstanding ye have well done that ye did communicate with my affliction. Now, ye Philippians, know also, that in the beginning of the Gospel, when I departed

* 1 Cor. ix. 3—14.

from Macedonia, *no church communicated with me as concerning giving and receiving,* BUT YE ONLY. For even in Macedonia ye sent once and again to my necessity. *Not because I desire a gift: but I desire fruit that may abound to your account."*

b.

1 Cor: xvi. 3, and 2 Cor: viii. 18. " When I come, *whomsoever ye shall approve by your letters,* them will I send to bring your liberality unto Jerusalem. And if it be meet that I go also, they shall go with me."
" We have sent with him (Titus,) the brother . . *who was chosen of the churches to travel with us* with this grace, which is administered by us to the glory of the same Lord, and declaration of your ready mind:— *avoiding this, that no man should blame us* in this abundance which is administered by us; *providing for honest things not only in the sight of the Lord, but* ALSO IN THE SIGHT OF MEN."

c.

Acts iii. 6., xx. 28. " Then Peter said, *silver and gold have I none:* but such as I have give I thee: In the name of Jesus Christ of Nazareth rise up and walk."
" Take heed unto yourselves, and to all the flock over the which the Holy Ghost hath made you overseers. . . . For I know this, that after my departing shall grievous wolves enter in among you, not sparing the flock. . . . . *I have coveted no man's silver, or gold, or apparel.* Yea, *ye yourselves know that these hands have ministered unto my necessities, and to them that were with me.* I have showed you all things, how that so labouring ye ought to support the weak, and to remember the words of the Lord Jesus, how he said, IT IS MORE BLESSED TO GIVE THAN TO RECEIVE."

Now, glancing the eye over the first of these quotations, (*a*) and the last two under No. III., it is easy to see that the apostle acted in money-matters, not only with great disinterestedness, but with marvellous circumspection, and with a constant eye to the questionable tendencies of that human nature with which he had to do, whose workings and characteristics he knew so well. In his measure, he, like his Master, "knew what was in man," and took care "not to commit himself to him," especially in matters in which pecuniary interests were concerned. He took an estimate, with keen discrimination, of those with whom he came in contact, and decided whom he could trust, and where he would be upon his guard. He could trust the Philippians—the descendants of Roman farmers and burghers, with something like plain honest English souls in them, —he let *them* deal with him as "concerning giving and receiving;" but he would not accept anything from the fickle and slippery Corinthians, though they owed him as much, and were far richer than the Macedonian Colonists. In each case he had his reward. In the one, opening his heart to them, years afterwards, when acknowledging a "second benefit,"—testifying to their former liberality, and telling them of the confidence accorded to them when they knew it not: in the other, being able to take his stand on the fact of never having touched a farthing of their money, when he was obliged to defend himself against unjust imputations. There is something refreshingly human in the way in which Paul deals with these rich but mean-souled Corinthians. How he scorns their insinuations; triumphantly appeals to his working for himself, or receiving and accepting aid from Macedonia,—anything rather than to take from *them!*—and how he even gives way to something like humour, asking, in a sort of satirical vein, " to be forgiven the wrong" of having saved them their money by not allowing himself to become burdensome to them!

Nor should we omit to notice, (*b*) how, with all his consciousness of uprightness, Paul did not choose to stand upon *that* in his money transactions as the agent of the churches. There are some people who are quite offended if, when entrusted with benevolent contributions, any thing is asked of them by way of security. Paul was superior to this littleness; in fact, he was too much of a man, and of a man of the world, not to feel that business was business, and ought to be ruled and regulated as such, between parties in the church and in relation to benevolent operations, as well as in secular society and in the concerns of ordinary life. He did not feel as if it were a suspicion or an insult if, having the money of others in his hands, his personal honour was not to be taken as a sufficient guarantee for its safe custody and proper application.

Or rather, it might be said, that though others might be satisfied to have it so, he would not allow it. No: he would have colleagues associated with him; the churches should appoint, so to speak, a joint treasurer; he required that the confidence placed in him should be extended to others, and that there might thus be the security of a shared responsibility. He had no fear of himself; he knew his own uprightness as ever living under the Divine eye; but that was not enough,—he would "avoid" the possibility of remark or suspicion, and have everything open and above board, so that, some one being authorized to act with him, provision would be made for what was honest and becoming, "not only in the sight of God, *but also in the sight of men.*"

Lastly, (c), Peter and John had neither silver nor gold that they could call their own, when they addressed the impotent man in the temple, though a few days before many had "sold their possessions and goods," and had committed the proceeds to their custody. Paul all his life worked hard and lived hard, and so he could say, as we have seen, towards the close of it, "I have coveted no man's silver, or gold, or apparel,—these hands have ministered to my necessities." Yes: Money may be capable of becoming "*a bad thing;*"—it may be so loved and used that it may taint the hand, and soil the soul, and corrupt the heart, and lead to other and even worse results;—But, most assuredly, if any men ever lived, who were careful that *it should never be a bad thing to them*, and who were determined to avoid in relation to it "even the *appearance* of evil," it was the Apostles of Him who said, "*Beware of covetousness;*" "Ye cannot serve God and Mammon."

PART SECOND.

Money may be put to a very Good Use.

LARGELY Thou givest, gracious Lord,
Largely Thy gifts should be restor'd ;
FREELY Thou givest, and Thy word
    Is, "FREELY GIVE."
He only, who forgets to hoard,
    Has learn'd to live.

                THE CHRISTIAN YEAR.

Sermon VII.

LUKE XVI. 9.

"Make to yourselves friends of the Mammon of unrighteousness; that, when ye fail, they may receive you into everlasting habitations."

FEW of you need to be reminded of what you have heard so often, that the two propositions which we drew from these words were these:— First, "that money may be a bad thing," but, secondly, "that it may be put to a very good use." On entering on this series of discourses, we stated it to be our intention to illustrate these two propositions, by collecting, arranging, and setting before you *all* that the New Testament contains relating to or bearing upon both. We limited ourselves to the New Testament,—in the first place, because it would be almost endless to gather together out of the Psalms, the Law, and the Prophets, all that they teach on the subject in question ; and, in the second place, because the New Testament, being received by the Christian Church as the last and most perfectly developed form of Divine thought and utterance, whatever *it* might be admitted to contain, would of course be accepted (or ought to be accepted) by Christian men as conclusive and final.

In the prosecution of our purpose, we have set before you whatever we could find in the New Testament illustrative of the first proposition, that "Money may be a bad thing." We had not to *prove* this exactly, since nobody doubts it. We might throw light upon it, however, and thus deepen a previous conviction. This we think we did, by a long line of very varied, and some of them very striking, illustrations. We now advance to the next thing we have to consider, namely, that, though "money may be a bad thing," it may nevertheless "*be put to a very good use.*" We have to sustain this statement by collecting and arranging what the New Testament says and teaches, in direct support of it, or by way of illustration.

Of course it will be understood, that by money being put "to a good use," we mean some use contemplated by secular or religious *beneficence*. You put money to a good use when you spend it appropriately and wisely on yourselves;—on your domestic comfort, the appointments of your houses, the education of your children;—on allowable recreation;—on journeys for enjoyment or health;—on books, or pictures, or works of art; on showing or returning friendly or family hospitalities. In these and various other ways money may be put to a good use. It is the privilege, rather indeed the duty, of those that have money to spend it,—provided, always, that they do this wisely, prudently, within proper limits, with a due regard to future provision for themselves and their children, and in accordance with the claims of benevolence and the obligations of religion. Quite recognizing, then, and admitting, that there are many ways in which money may be put to a good use by spending it, and spending it upon yourselves; yet, what we have properly to do with in a religious argument, is the good use that money may be put to *by* GIVING ;—by devoting it to and so employing it for *the benefit of others*, that the parting with it is a gratuity, benevolence, donation, or whatever you may please to call it,—as distinct from what is *spent* in the way of purchase and payment.

Now, as a preliminary remark, I beg to say, that I can quite understand that any statement in favour of the religious or benevolent use of money by *giving it away*—and especially the idea of this being of ultimate advantage to the giver—may be met, at the outset, by protest and objection. Some would say, that to give money at all, is a social and political mistake; that anything in the form of charitable provision, for individuals or classes, creates far more misery than it relieves; that the hope of pecuniary, or other help, in nine cases out of ten prevents people from helping themselves, encourages improvidence, and destroys independence. The whole thing, it may be said, is a blunder. It is contrary to the advanced views and demonstrated conclusions of social science. As to the idea of connecting with the religious employment of money any advantages or benefits to be reaped by the individual, *especially in a future world*, that would, of course, be rejected by others as rank Popery,—as what involved the notion of human merit, the merit of good works, and was inconsistent with the fundamental principle of Protestantism— justification by faith. I can quite conceive, that these and other objections should start up, in different minds, on the mere announcement of the subject which lies before us. I wish, therefore, to say at once, that when the proper time comes, we shall be quite willing to weigh whatever may be offered in opposition to our argument; but that, as our proposed object is, *simply to ascertain what the New Testament teaches on the subject*, it becomes us, first of all, to find out *that :*—to find it out, by collecting its statements, and listening to their import, and taking them to mean whatever they may say. We must neither interpret them by any scientific hypothesis, nor refuse to recognize their manifest meaning from the fear of clashing with theological conclusions. What we have first to do then, is, as I have said, to set forth before our minds—fully, clearly, honestly—what appears to be the teaching of Christ and His Apostles on the good uses to which money may be put by a Christian man;—its use, that is to say, not merely as to the purposes to which it may be devoted, but, (what seems the meaning of the text) *as to the beneficial results which may flow from that devotement to the man himself.* When we have got the teaching of the New Testament thus fairly before us, we can then consider how it is to be dealt with;—whether it is to be accepted in its absolute meaning and pure literality; or whether it is to be modified by other truths; or whether it is to be regarded as no longer binding,—as having in it Jewish or other elements which could not but appear in the first years of the new Dispensation, but which were meant to be superseded and to pass away as the *spirit* of that Dispensation was gradually developed, and as everything connected with the individual and the race—this world and the next—came to be seen and understood in the light of it. If any feel that they must go further than this, and that, finding the New Testament to teach what they are obliged to reject as unscientific and injurious, they are led to doubt the Divine claims of Christianity itself, why, they will not expect us to sympathise with such doubts, whatever difficulty we may feel in meeting or allaying them.

Leaving all this, however, for the present;—remembering that our first business is, not to defend the law, but *to find it out,*—to ascertain and exhibit what the Book actually says, irrespective of consequences,—disregarding alike the foregone conclusions of both philosophers and divines,—we proceed to do that.

I.

The New Testament teaches, *that the pious and charitable employment of money—the giving of the money itself, or of what it represents—in the way of kindly and beneficent action,* IS ONE OF THE REQUIRED FORMS OF CHRISTIAN OBEDIENCE.

The words "alms" and "almsgiving" have become distasteful to us, from religious and social considerations; from the doctrinal and practical evils which have resulted from the abuse of the things. But the perversion of a thing, is not only not in itself a sufficient reason for setting it aside,—but it is to be remembered, that the fact of *perversion* implies the existence, perhaps the obligation, of the thing itself. Besides, in the present case, we may regard "alms" and "almsgiving" not in the gross or familiar acceptation of giving money to professional beggars and street mendicants, but simply as words involving the principle of pecuniary liberality in whatever form wisdom and experience shall prescribe as expedient. So understood, there need be no fear of the things, and there ought to be no prejudice against the words. *We*, at any rate, have no option, for, as they meet us among the primary utterances of the Great Teacher, when announcing, in the Sermon on the Mount, the laws of the kingdom, we must take them as they stand there, remembering that what *He* says, and says with authority, it is not for us to question but to accept.

Our Lord, then, found the exercise of pecuniary liberality existing among the Jews in the form of " almsgiving ;"—something expressive at once of humanity and piety,—kindness towards the poor, and obedience to God. He found this in existence as a recognized thing; as a duty and service supposed to be prescribed both by Patriotism and faith ; and we gather from His words that *He accepted it*. He took the thing itself—the central obligation and principle—He approved, adopted, and enforced it, while He condemned and stigmatized the perversions and abuses by which it had come to be disfigured. " Take heed that *ye do not your alms* before men to be seen of them." " *When thou doest thine alms*, do not sound a trumpet before thee, as the hypocrites do in the synagogues and in the streets, that they may have glory of men." " But, *when thou doest alms* let not thy left hand know what thy right hand doeth, that *thine alms may be in secret*."*
Nothing can be plainer than this language. While

* Math. vi. 1—4.

it condemns the ostentation which too often accompanied the exercise of pecuniary liberality in our Lord's time, it distinctly recognizes the obligation and propriety of the thing itself. Our Lord takes for granted that the duty will be done—that money will be given in the form of considerate kindness to the poor,—but He regulates the *manner* in which it is to be carried out. " *When* thou doest thine alms, &c." as if He had said,—"I assume that thou wilt thus act. I do not forbid it. I do not condemn the practice,—yea, rather, I recognize it as right and enforce it as obligatory. I say not, cease from the thing,—give it up altogether,—*don't do it*. I only say don't do it *after a wrong fashion*. Take heed to the spirit and the manner of the act. Do it,—but do it as before God, not with a view to be seen of men." This is obviously the import of our Lord's utterances. They condemn the perversion and abuse ; but they recognize the obligation and the law. They strip off the temporary and accidental in the forms and modes of the time then present : but they leave in its integrity what is central and substantial, accepting it as moral and permanent. "Do thine alms quietly, modestly; without show and noise; without self-consciousness, even, or complacent recollection,—neither doing them before others nor talking of them to thyself. Do them in secret, humbly, devoutly, before God ; but *do* them,—for they are to be done. The thing itself is right, though some may do it in a wrong way. *I say unto you, take heed as to both;* do the right thing in the right way; for the thing is to be done and I take it for granted that my disciples will do it."

But our Lord did more than this. He not only *constructively*, and by necessary implication, recognized and enforced the duty of pecuniary beneficence, but He said so directly and positively,—in so many words,—and words too, singularly suggestive. He not only gave directions about the *mode*, thus *implying* a recognition of the thing; but He insisted on the thing itself,—requiring that it should be attended to as a part of our moral and religious obedience. Hence, He not only says, "*When* you give alms" do so and so; but He says "give" them,—"*give alms of such things as you have*," *—adding a reason for the injunction, or an encouragement to obey it, which will come to be considered in its proper place.

The observation just made applies to the text lying before us, from which this series of discourses started. "*I say unto you, make to yourselves friends of the mammon of unrighteousness;*"—do kindnesses, confer favours upon others, through the thoughtful and considerate employment of money. This is the injunction. It stands there as a law. The result that may follow, which is next suggested as a motive or

* Luke xi. 41; xii. 33.

encouragement, will have to be looked at and explained by-and-by.

In addition to those things it may be remembered, that the only unquestionable tradition which has come down to us from the lifetime of our Lord, and which enshrines a sentiment said to be His, is a sentence bearing upon this very subject. The address of St. Paul to the elders at Miletus concludes, you remember, with these words,—" I have showed you all things, how that so labouring ye ought to support the weak, and to remember the words of the Lord Jesus, how he said, *It is more blessed to give than to receive.*" * These words, framed into that sentence, are not to be met with in any of the Gospels, though the sentiment is no doubt there in other phraseology. But it is not to be doubted that St. Paul refers to a distinct and distinctly remembered *saying* of Christ which was handed down among the disciples. The words, as he repeated them, had been uttered by Jesus; and though not recorded by any of His biographers, they were held by the believers in constant remembrance. They were referred to as a maxim and a law. Once spoken by Jesus, they fell not from His lips as lost, though no scribe was to write them in the record of His discourses! They were caught up, as it were, by the surrounding atmosphere as a precious possession; they were retained in it, and

* Acts xx. 35.

secured, and became endowed with a ceaseless and diffusive activity; the echo of them was heard, and was listened to with delight, as it spread through the years of the Apostolic age; it has gone on reverberating ever since, as it will go on throughout all time, the only authentic and unquestionable *tradition* of the Church. Whatever the Master's contemporaries forgot of His conversation or discourse, there was one thing which was tenaciously remembered and fondly recalled,—a divine sentence, which will ever be associated with the name of the Lord Jesus, for "wherever the Gospel shall be preached, this shall be spoken for a memorial of Him," that *He said,*— "IT IS MORE BLESSED TO GIVE THAN TO RECEIVE."

II.

The same idea—the idea, that is to say, of pecuniary liberality, or what amounts to it, being regarded and recognized as one of the required forms of Christian obedience—is to be met with, expressed, or implied, in several passages contained in the Epistles. "If a brother or sister be naked, and destitute of daily food, and one of you say unto them, Depart in peace; be ye warmed and filled; notwithstanding *ye give them not* those things which are needful to the body; what doth it profit?" * "Let us not love in word, neither

* James ii. 15, 16.

in tongue, but *in deed and in truth*,"*—that is, by act and service;—by the work of the hands, and not merely the fruit of the lip;—by giving money, or money's worth, where necessity requires it. "He that says he loves God and hates his brother"—not showing his love by positive acts, if it be in the power of his hand to do them—"is a liar," † and nothing else; for, "as the body without the spirit is dead," so, either "faith" or feeling "without works is dead also." ‡

"*Bear ye one another's burdens; and so fulfil the law of Christ.*" § The "law of Christ" may refer to the whole of His teaching, to the sum of what He requires of us in the way of obedience; and the spirit that pervades it may be supposed to be exemplified in the "bearing of one another's burdens." Perhaps, however, we have here a special allusion to what our Lord called "His new commandment." The old commandment was, "thou shalt love thy neighbour as thyself;" Christ's new commandment is, "thou shalt love thy brother better than thyself;"—for His words are, "a new commandment give I unto you, that ye love one another;"—that ye love one another "*as I have loved you;*" ‖ which is expounded by St. John to mean, that, "as He laid down His life for us, we ought to be ready to lay down our lives for the brethren." ¶ Many things

* 1 John iii. 18. † 1 John iv. 20. ‡ James ii. 16 and 26.
§ Gal. vi. 2.   ‖ John xv. 12.   ¶ 1 John iii. 16.

short of that, however, may be a fulfilling of the law of Christ. The text quoted says, that "bearing one another's burdens" may be that, and we all know how that may be done. How, not only by sympathy, by kindly recollection, and loving speech, and wise counsel a helping hand may be given to a man, to ease the burden pressing on his shoulders; but what a load may sometimes be lifted from the heart, and how the paralyzed spirit may spring up nimble and elastic, by the gift of fifty or the loan of a hundred pounds!

That the exercise of kind feeling, of benevolent sympathy, manifesting itself in positive acts, and these acts sometimes taking the form of pecuniary help,—that this is an essential part of the obedience of a Christian man, and necessary to the completeness of a saintly character, is *implied* in various ways in other passages. As, for instance, when "*love*," "*goodness*," "*beneficence*," and similar virtues are enumerated among "the fruits of the Spirit,"*—the results and evidences of regeneration.—When the believers are exhorted "to *put on*, as the elect of God, *bowels and mercies*,"† that is, to encourage and cultivate charitable affections, till their visible expression shall clothe and adorn them like a beautiful garment. —When it is said, "if there be any consolation in Christ, if any comfort of love, if any fellowship

* Gal. v. 22. † Col. iii. 12.

of the spirit, if any bowels and mercies, fulfil ye my joy;"—"look not every man on his own things,"—his own wants, wishes, interests and satisfactions—"but every man also on the things of others"—on *their* wants, circumstances, and need; —"Let this mind be in you which was also in Christ Jesus," "who, though He was rich, yet for your sakes became poor, that ye through His poverty might be rich."* The same thing is involved whenever the idea of stewardship is presented; and especially when presented in connexion with the material instrument of beneficence. "Use hospitality one to another without grudging. As every man hath received the gift, even so minister the same one toward another, as good stewards of the manifold grace of God." † The "*manifold* grace"—or the *diversified* gifts—referred to here, include the bestowments of Providence, as well as the donations of the Spirit;—the power to do good by pecuniary beneficence, as well as to edify the church by instructive discourse. Hence, "hospitality" is mentioned, which some, by the property with which God had entrusted them, were much more able to exercise than others. The "well-beloved Gaius," to whom St. John addresses his third epistle, was a man, we may suppose, in good circumstances. He regarded his wealth as the gift of God, bestowed upon him to enable him to be

* Philip. ii. 1—5. 2 Cor. viii. 9. † 1 Peter iv. 9, 10.

useful; and he was a good steward who employed it as one "who was to give an account." Hence, says the apostle, "thou doest faithfully whatever thou doest to the brethren and to strangers; who have borne witness to thy charity before the Church; whom if thou bring forward on their journey after a godly sort, thou shalt do well. Because that for His name's sake they went forth, taking nothing of the Gentiles. We therefore ought to receive such, that we might be fellow helpers to the truth."* In all this, you observe, there is the apostolic recognition of the saying, that "property has its duties as well as its rights." To employ it liberally, in beneficent deeds, is a matter of positive obligation. To do this is to do what "*ought*" to be done; to act "well" and "faithfully," "worthy of God," as a conscientious servant and a good steward.

But the idea we have been illustrating is set forth in the most distinct and emphatic form, in the explicit exhortation of St. Paul to Timothy:—"Charge them that are rich in this world, that they be not highminded, nor trust in uncertain riches, but in the living God, who giveth us richly all things to enjoy: *that they do good,—that they be rich in good works, —ready to distribute,—willing to communicate.*" † Nothing can be plainer or more imperative than this. To put money to a good use, by employing it in beneficent acts, is here recognized as a part of Chris-

* 3 John 5—8 † 1 Tim. vi. 17, 18.

tian obedience; and not only so,—not only is it a duty incumbent on the rich, but it is one in which they should *abound,* and *towards* which they should cultivate a constant readiness, as to that which specially belongs to them. " God loveth a *cheerful* giver,"—one who is not forced by constraint and necessity,—and He expects a correspondence between what He has bestowed and what is accomplished. Hence, He "who maketh rich " by " giving power to get wealth,"—and who, in addition to that, has enriched the soul by making it the partaker of " precious faith,"—requires of those who are thus distinguished, —who *have* the money, and who *profess* to have the principle,—that " they do good, be rich in good works,—ready to distribute,—willing to communicate;" forward to embrace and glad to welcome every call and opportunity of usefulness, so far as obligation extends,—which is so far as their ability permits. God does not expect " to reap where he has not sown, nor to gather where He has not strewed." He does not require "what a man has not," nor does He look for much where He has given little. But He does require much where much has been given;—He does look for returns " *according to that which a man hath.*" *

* 1 Cor. viii. 12

III.

We conclude this survey of proofs and illustrations of the position we advanced, by returning again to where we started,—listening to the words of the Lord Himself in His sermon on the Mount. From Him we learn, that the duty of doing good, as a Christian obligation, is not to be limited to the "household of faith." *There* it may meet with its first objects, and be exercised in connexion with a special affection; but it is not to be confined there;— it is to pass over the limits of the peculiar brotherhood, and is not always to be careful about the worthiness and desert of those whom it benefits. The spirit of this was caught and manifested by the two chief and representative apostolic men,—the Apostle of the Gentiles, and the Apostle of the Circumcision; the one praying that Christians "might increase and abound in love towards *one another* and *towards all men;*"[*] and the other crowning his catalogue of Christian virtues by the two graces of "brotherly kindness," and *universal* " *charity.*"[†]

Our Lord says, that by an ample and all embracing *beneficence*—not merely the culture of a sentiment, but the doing of deeds—deeds of kindness to men as men,—we shall approach nearest to the imitation of God, whom He depicts as the supreme and universal

[*] 1 Thess. iii. 12.   [†] 2 Peter i. 5—7.

philanthropist. " Give to him that asketh of thee, and from him that would borrow of thee, turn not thou away. Love your enemies, bless them that curse you, do good to them that hate you ;—*that you may be the children of your father who is in heaven:* for *He* maketh His sun to rise on the evil and on the good, and sendeth rain on the just and on the unjust."*—Our Lord when He said this was sitting upon the Mount: there were spread before Him the possessions of a number of persons, doubtless of great variety of character; the sun at the moment might be pouring his warmth and glory on them all. Accustomed as He was to connect His precepts with sensible images, He probably pointed to the prospect while He pronounced the injunctions. He thus illustrated His teaching by a fact, by the *visible* proof of God's universal providential beneficence, and then He concluded this portion of His discourse, telling them to imitate what they then saw, by the mysteriously pregnant and suggestive words—" be ye, therefore, perfect, even as your father who is in heaven is perfect."

IV.

We have thus, I think, established the proposition, which was laid down at the commencement of the discourse, and which constitutes the basis of this

* Math. v. 45.

part of our argument, namely, "that the New Testament teaches, that the pious and charitable employment of money—the giving of the money itself, or of what it represents—in the way of kindly and beneficent action, is one of the required forms of Christian obedience." This is only the first link in a regular series of successive propositions, which will be brought before you, none of which, however, will require for their exposition more than *a portion* of any future discourse. For the present, we close the argument at this first step. We do not, as yet, enter into the objections which some might oppose to what we teach. Just now, as I said before, we have to *ascertain* the law, not to defend it. If, indeed, what is made out *be* the law of the New Testament, I don't know that it becomes one to attempt to defend it. If a thing be admitted to be God's truth, it is not a matter to be questioned but obeyed. It stands on authority before which we bow down and are willing to be silent;—even to receive by faith what we may not be able to apprehend by the understanding; quite certain that God can see the wisdom and propriety of whatever He prescribes, and will sustain and defend His own truth.

We may just say one last word, in the form of meeting a suggested objection, though it may perhaps anticipate what may have to be done at a future time·

The thought may possibly have occurred to some of you, as our argument proceeded, that, if what we were saying was the Christian doctrine respecting the beneficent uses of money, it would, if fully carried out, fill the world with dependants and paupers; destroy the manly spirit of the poor, and multiply the scenes of misery and helplessness which are to be met with in Popish countries, or wherever there are established charitable endowments. To this sort of feeling I only answer at present, that it may perhaps be apparent, before we have done, that the law of the New Testament, taken as a whole—one part being allowed to supplement another—is furnished with safeguards against its abuse. There is no danger of bad consequences flowing from the inculcation of what we have advanced, if the *whole* of the Divine teaching be fully adhered to. The spirit of the book is broadly condemnatory of any mean or calculating mendicant who would take advantage of its law of beneficence. The law, it is to be observed, is binding upon *all*. The obligation is *to give*, not to receive. And that Christian men may be able to do this, even the most humble, they are commanded " to work, labouring with their hands, that they may *have* something to give to him that needeth,"* and may be at once independent and liberal. "*If any will not work*,"—then it is ordered that " *he shall not eat*."† If able-bodied, and having

* Eph. iv. 28. † 2 Thess. iii. 10; 1 Thess. iv. 11, 12.

fair opportunity of employment, but shirking it from idleness and disposed to spunge on the kindness of the beneficent,—that kindness is arrested,—the supplies are stopped,—and the indolent are told that if they will not labour for their living and earn their dinner, *they may go without it.* A spirit of high and honourable independence is inculcated by the Scriptures, properly understood. It lives in the precepts and is exemplified in the conduct of apostolic men. It is embodied, as we shall see, in the social regulations and pecuniary arrangements of the primitive church. Christians, if really such, will never be beggars because they are saints, or presume to think that those who are saints are bound to support them.

Sermon VIII.

LUKE XVI. 9.

"Make to yourselves friends of the mammon of unrighteousness; that when ye fail, they may receive you into everlasting habitations."

AFTER largely illustrating the first proposition which these words suggest, that money "may be a bad thing," seeing that it is here described as the Mammon of unrighteousness; we proceeded in our last discourse, to discuss and illustrate our second proposition, namely, "that, nevertheless, it may be put to a very good use."

We explained that the good use of money with which *we* had to do, was, of course, not its innocent or laudable *secular* employment—its being wisely expended on ourselves or our families,—but its religious or benevolent use, in the way of *giving*,—of donation, or gratuity, for the benefit of others—to mitigate physical want, or to sustain and strengthen any form of philanthropic or religious agency.

After stating that we should leave certain anticipated objections to be dealt with hereafter, we proceeded to do *the one thing*, which, first of all, it becomes us to attempt,—namely, to ascertain exactly *all* that the New Testament says upon the subject. What we want to know is, the teaching of the New Testament in respect to the giving of money;—the way in which the thing is dealt with,—the ground on which it is put,—the motives by which it is enforced, —with anything else that may throw light upon it— its obligation or results—to be found in The Book, the gospels and epistles, the sayings of our Lord and the writings of the Apostles.

We intimated that we should collect and arrange the different passages which in any way bore on the matter in hand; and that we should set these before you, under a series of connected propositions; which propositions would thus become so many links in a chain of illustrative argument that might lead us to some distinct and definite conclusion. The first, only, of these propositions was stated and supported in our last discourse. We now propose to advance to the remainder, or to so many of them as our limited time may permit us to touch.

The first proposition, which we largely supported last Sunday from every part of the New Testament, was this;—" that the pious and charitable employment of money—the giving of the money itself, or of what money represents—in the way of kind and beneficent deeds, is one of the required forms of

Christian obedience."—The proof of this, that beneficence is a *duty*,—that it rests upon us as an obligation,—is enforced by the laws of the kingdom, —and is expected as the natural fruit of a true and living Christian faith,—the *proof* of this, we found in every part of the New Testament, from the sayings of Jesus on the Mount, to the closing words of St. John, the last of the Apostles. We now connect with our first proposition, a second, which we express in the following words:—"*This duty*, this required form of religious obedience, *is represented, when done, as something which is especially acceptable and pleasing to God.*"

" God is love, and he that loveth, dwelleth in God, and God in him." But the love of God is energetic and active; it is proved and manifested by works. His nature is an everflowing and overflowing fountain of good. " He giveth to all liberally and upbraideth not." " He has not left Himself without witness, seeing that He giveth to all, life, and breath, and all things,—filling their mouths with food and gladness." He delights to communicate. He gives constantly, everywhere, and with a divine and affluent liberality. "He opens His hand, and satisfieth the desire of every living thing." " From Him cometh down every good, and every perfect gift." It is the glory of His intelligent offspring to be like Him;—to be loving and beneficent, as *He* is ;—to have in them the *principle* of which kind and gracious acts are the visible expression, and, so clearly to express it *by* such acts, that the proof of its being in them shall be patent and complete. Now, these acts—which are at once the proof of this internal God-likeness, and constitute one of the forms of action likest God's—is not only, as we showed last Sunday, a mode of required obedience, but (as we now proceed to show) is one which, when rendered, is spoken of as peculiarly pleasant and acceptable.

I.

"*To do good and to communicate, forget not; for with such sacrifices God is well pleased.*"* In this passage, the general expression "to do good"—a thing which may be accomplished in many ways—is connected with a particular form of it, with "*communicating,*" that is, with positive beneficent acts; giving something to others in the way of benevolent help; —imparting, from what you have to spare, to their want and necessity. That is the thing, or the class of things, enjoined. But observe how the motive or inducement to obedience which is here added, elevates and beautifies these things. They are termed "sacrifices," and such sacrifices as those "with which

* Heb. xiii. 16.

God is well pleased." The word need not imply that they are always sacrifices to *us*, in the sense of requiring painful self-denial—though sometimes they may include that; but the word does imply that they are *offered to God*,—that they are the expression of religious principle, as well as the result of natural sentiment,—that they are offered as *designed* obedience, and are not merely the outcome of an unintelligent impulse. When thus rendered they become divine; they partake of the nature of sacred acts. The individual is beheld as if he stood at an altar, and was engaged in the highest religious service. He discharges the office of a priest;—his benevolent work is accepted as worship:—wherever done, the place is a temple and the presentation a sacrifice! And "with such sacrifices God is well pleased." No language can more strongly express than this, the peculiar acceptableness of Christian beneficence; and especially so, when you remember the sacred associations with which such language would be employed by a Jew. Sacrifice was the highest act of the Hebrew worship; it could only be acceptably performed at one place,—and only by the official assistance of the consecrated sons of Aaron; and still further, if anything was brought that was maimed or imperfect, blind or blemished, such sacrifices were an abomination and an offence. The apostle knew all this; even as a Christian it had to him a solemn significance, so that, when his language suggests to us the idea of a Christian man standing before the altar as a consecrated priest, and presenting a sacrifice with which God is well pleased, he has used the highest and most emphatic form of expression which to him was possible, to set forth the greatness and acceptableness of the service.

The same idea is presented in another passage, which is often very much misunderstood and perverted. "*Pure religion before God even the Father is this,—to visit the fatherless and widow in their affliction; and to keep ourselves unspotted from the world.*"* This is sometimes supposed to mean that *religion itself*—the *essence* and *substance* of it—consists in kind and charitable deeds. But that is not the meaning.—The word rendered "religion," in this text, does not refer to the inward principle, but to the outward embodiment of it. It implies the existence of a spiritual life, which becomes visible by what is described. The word means literally religious *service*,—the service of a priest, or priesthood, in things pertaining to God. This divine service requires a divine man,—the *inner* man, the man within the heart, who is born of God. This spiritual man, a believing, regenerated human soul, has to live and act, to serve and work; and his work is a priestly function, and his service a perpetual worship; he has

* James i. 27.

to appear daily in his sacred, official robes, which are to consist of these personal, divine virtues, which in the sight of God are of great price. As the dress of Aaron was for glory and beauty, symbolizing spiritual ideas, so the Christian priest is to exhibit in himself the grace and the truth by putting on the garments of purity and benevolence,—"by keeping himself unspotted from the world, and by visiting the fatherless and widows in their affliction." These two things, thus particularly specified, are intended to express what is comprehensive and general;—all sanctity and all virtue,—inward purification and outward obedience. And, that kindness and beneficence—visiting and relieving the fatherless and widows—that *this* should be seen to stand where it is, and do what it does, in this suggestive picture of religious service, is another proof of its value and acceptableness in the sight of God.

The idea we are illustrating, of beneficent acts being regarded as "sacrifices well-pleasing to God," is carried on in another passage, and carried further than we have yet had it. There is added to the image of the altar and the priest—the visible service of the earthly temple,—what takes place "within the vail;"—the effect, so to speak, of the presented offering on Him who receives it. True, this idea is involved in the phrase "well-pleasing to God," which occurred in the passage first quoted; and the same phrase will be heard again in that which we are about to quote; but in this next one, you will observe, that the *literal* expression is aggravated and intensified by a figurative allusion which we have not had before, and which adds greatly to its compass and force. The passage in question may be thus introduced :—The Apostle Paul, when a prisoner at Rome, was in great destitution. From some cause or other, he was neglected or opposed by the Christians of the place; of whom he says, "all sought their own, not the things that were Jesus Christ's," and some of whom designedly and deliberately endeavoured to annoy him, and sought "to add affliction to his bonds." Under these circumstances, the members of the Church at Philippi, his first and favourite European converts, made a money collection, or sent to him a supply of useful and necessary articles; and this benevolence he gratefully acknowledges in the letter which he wrote to them on the return of the messenger by whom their gift was sent. The language he employs illustrates at once the character of the man, and the light in which he viewed, and in which he teaches us to view, a beneficent act in its relation to God. "I rejoiced in the Lord greatly, that now at the last your care of me hath flourished again : wherein ye were also careful but ye lacked opportunity. Not that I speak in respect of want, for I have learned, in whatever state I am, therewith to be content. . . .

Notwithstanding, ye have well done, that ye did communicate with my affliction.—Not that I desire a gift; but I desire fruit that may abound to your account. But I have all and abound, I am full, having received of Epaphroditus the things which were sent from you, AN ODOUR OF A SWEET SMELL, *a sacrifice acceptable, well-pleasing to God.*"* In these words there is added to the simple idea of sacrifice, or a presentation to God, a further allusion to the burning of incense, and to the action of the fire that consumes the offering,—which together throw off what fills the air with a divine perfume, and which is figuratively regarded as ascending to heaven and producing a similar result there. It is a strong, sensible image, intended to express the peculiar complacency with which God regards loving and beneficent deeds,— the condescending satisfaction with which He accepts them. It reminds us of the language of the Old Testament, and of the way in which the first sacrifice after the flood, offered by the second father of the race, was received and commemorated:—"and Noah builded an altar unto the Lord; and took of every clean beast, and of every clean fowl, and offered burnt-offerings upon the altar. And *the Lord smelled a sweet savour;* and the Lord said in His heart, I will not again curse the ground any more for man's sake .... while the earth remaineth,

* Philip. iv. 10—18.

seed time and harvest, and cold and heat, and summer and winter, shall not cease."

II.

The subject may be further illustrated by referring to one or two facts in the personal history of our Lord Jesus Christ. There is a revelation of God in the heavens and the earth;—in the phenomena of nature, and the constitution of man. But the highest manifestation of the Divine, is to be seen in Him who was "The Lord from heaven." "The Word was made flesh, and dwelt amongst us; and we beheld His glory, the glory of the only begotten of the Father, full of grace and truth." "In Him dwelt all the fulness of the Godhead bodily." "God spake by," and revealed Himself to us in, "His Son," "who is the brightness of His glory, and the express image of His person." Through Jesus Christ, we have such a manifestation of God in the flesh, that He said of Himself, "*he that hath seen Me hath seen the Father*." So strongly do we feel this, that we listen to the loving words of Jesus—contemplate His acts of compassion and mercy—treasure in our hearts His forbearance with the froward, and His encouragement to the penitent—and see in His human tenderness and tears—what lifts us to the consolatory persuasion and assurance that there is something in

God Himself answering to and corresponding with all this. We are of course warranted in applying the same principle to the manner in which He graciously accepted, and was "well pleased" with, those expressions of love which came to Him in the form of beneficent donations. We cannot doubt that the way in which He received well meant hospitable attentions, and the contributions of those who "ministered to Him of their substance,"* was indicative of a benignant complacency,—as we know that He noticed slight or forgetfulness, where, in connexion with a show of respect, there was the absence of customary courtesies. "Simon, I have somewhat to say unto thee . . . . I entered into thy house, thou gavest me no water for my feet, but this woman hath washed my feet with tears, and wiped them with the hairs of her head. Thou gavest me no kiss; but she, since the time I came in, hath not ceased to kiss my feet. My head with oil thou didst not anoint, but she hath anointed my feet with ointment."† Now, apart from every thing else in this incident, and in the application which our Lord makes of its circumstances to higher spiritual truth, there is *this* truth underlying His words, that He was not insensible to kindnesses done to Him,—and that, while He noticed deficiency in substance or mode, He accepted with pleasure, and felt and expressed a

* Luke viii. 3. † Luke vii. 40—46.

personal satisfaction in such acts of attention and liberality as proved and manifested grateful love.

But this personal appreciation of kindness—and of kindness which was *literally* costly and expensive—was more fully displayed on another and more memorable occasion. Jesus was in Bethany, in the house of Simon the leper.* Simon had received good at His hands, having been cured by Him of a disease which excluded him from society. Being able now to partake of social enjoyments, he made a supper, and bade many, inviting our Lord and His disciples to the feast. Our Lord went, willing at once to give pleasure and to receive it,—though His mind was then entering within the shadow of the cloud whose terrible darkness was soon to overwhelm Him. In the midst of the entertainment, a loving woman rose noiselessly from her seat;—she had in her hand "an alabaster box of very precious ointment," "ointment of spikenard, very costly;"—approaching Jesus, she broke the box and poured its contents on His head and feet! The company was startled, and "the room was filled with the odour of the ointment." It was worth much. It might have been sold for three hundred pence,—nearly ten pounds of our money. It had no doubt been long thought of, and the purchase prepared for by much saving and self-sacrifice. It was an expensive gift. The disciples murmured. They thought

* Math. xxvi. 6—13.

it waste. They talked about the claims of the poor, and began to calculate how much good might have been done if the money had been devoted to ordinary charity. "But Jesus said unto them, *Let her alone. Why trouble ye the woman?*" *His* care for the poor was not, we are certain, less than theirs; but He wished to teach His disciples that there are other virtues besides giving to the poor,—other modes of devoting property to God besides that of literal almsgiving. And to show that with *such* sacrifices "God is well pleased," *He*, "in whom they might see the Father," proceeded to express His personal complacency in this expensive expression of love towards Himself. "Let her alone; for she hath wrought a good work upon *me*." "The poor ye have always with you, and whensoever ye will, ye may do them good; but me ye have not always." "Verily I say unto you, wheresoever this gospel shall be preached in the whole world, there shall this, that this woman hath done, be told for a memorial of her." The sacrifice was accepted. Just as the "odour of the ointment" was pleasant to the sense, the beneficent act was itself productive of an inward satisfaction. Nor can we doubt, but that the saying of Jesus that the good work wrought upon Him was accepted as an anointing preparatory "to His burial," had its influence in stimulating the liberality of others, when, a few days afterwards, it was thought necessary

THE WIDOW'S MITE. 179

that "sweet spices" should be "brought" to anoint "His body."* In addition to what three of the women purchased, the disciple that came to Jesus by night had provided "a mixture of myrrh and aloes, of about an hundred pounds weight."† The one Mary did "what she could;" the two others with Salome followed her example. Joseph and Nicodemus brought of their abundance. The gifts of all were acceptable as sacrifice and fragrant as incense in *His* sight, whose will it is, that "all men should honour the Son, even as they honour the Father."

Two concluding references to our Lord's sayings, will close these illustrative proofs of the acceptableness to God of loving and beneficent acts. Sitting one day over against the treasury, as the people were going into the temple, Jesus observed a poor widow casting in "two mites, which make a farthing."‡ There were many that gave much; but to the eye of Jesus no gift was so large or so liberal as hers. She "gave all she had, even all her living." She was a poor widow; but she thought of others that might be poorer than herself. "In a great trial of affliction," (and few trials are greater than widowhood,) her "deep poverty abounded unto the riches of her liberality." The act did not pass unnoticed. Our Lord observed it; spoke of it; praised it. In His sight such a good deed, in this evil world, shone

* Mark xvi. 1.   † John xix. 39.   ‡ Mark xii. 41.

like a star! It was grateful and acceptable; and again, we say, "in *Him* we see the Father."

But the most convincing proof of the position we are illustrating, is to be found in our Lord's description of what is to take place "when the Son of man shall come in His glory, and there shall be gathered before Him all nations."* To what event this may refer, supposing it to be uncertain, is of no moment to us in this argument. The point we have to notice is just the same under any explanation or on any hypothesis. Those whose conduct is referred to with approval, are those who were distinguished by beneficent deeds;—who fed the hungry, clothed the naked, cared for the stranger, visited the sick, remembered and relieved prisoners and captives. The Son of man, on the throne of His glory, identifies himself with the objects of their benevolence, and tells them that whatever they did to *them* they did to *Him*. No words, equal to these, can possibly be imagined to express the acceptableness of kindness and liberality —distributing and communicating to the necessities of others—as one of the forms of Christian obedience. " Well pleasing," indeed, must that be, of which it is to be said—and said in the audience of all worlds— "*Inasmuch as ye did it to one of the least of these my brethren*, YE DID IT UNTO ME."

---

* Math. xxv. 31—40

We have thus set before you the New Testament proofs and illustrations of our second proposition. The first was, "That beneficent acts are an essential and required part of Christian obedience;" they are matter of obligation, and are prescribed by law. The second proposition is, "That these acts, thus enforced and commanded, are, when properly rendered, a service peculiarly acceptable to God." This statement we have shown to be true, by quotations from the apostolic letters,—by illustrative facts in our Lord's life,—and by sayings of His in conversation or discourse. We might now advance to our third proposition—the next link in our chain of argument; but, for the sake of avoiding misapprehension, I think it may be well to add here two or three explanatory remarks as to some things which it is important to keep in mind.

III.

Recollect, then, in the first place, that, while in this argument we have to do with what we speak of as *beneficent acts* under the idea of *the giving of money*, it is not to be understood that the import of the language is to be limited to that. There are many ways of doing a kind thing, besides that of pecuniary help. In fact, we all know that that may not only often be the least useful, and the least satisfactory to the individual served, but that it may be given from inward disinclination *to do something that would be far more valuable.* To devote time and thought to another's concerns, and to aid him by some sort of personal effort, would be often of far more use than to give him a cheque, or to make him an advance. But rather than do this,—and even rather than put themselves to a trifling inconvenience, by giving up a dinner-party, or rising an hour or two sooner than usual,—there are men who would part with a considerable sum, and part with it gladly, to escape the necessity of a little personal sacrifice, and who would then soothe themselves with the thought that they had done a very handsome and friendly thing! This is a strong case, and is looked at from a worldly point of view; but it illustrates a principle,—and one, too, which operates in the Church, and among Christian men, as well as in the world. We are quite aware, then, be it understood, that there are far more valuable modes of beneficence than that in which money is concerned;—and that a kind word, an encouraging look, a sympathizing visit, the devotion of time to unravel a difficulty and to give advice, may be of more worth to a man than "thousands of gold and silver." We quite understand that. Nevertheless, seeing that the Scripture *does* specify money-contributions, and money-help, in its "good deeds" and acceptable "sacrifices,"—sacrifices that are "well pleasing to God,"—seeing that these may be fairly *included* among the forms of service which beneficence may assume in the diversified action of a Christian man,—we are perfectly justified in referring to these as constituting *a part* of Christian obedience. The true statement of the matter is just this :—that the benevolent use of money is *one* of the ways in which Christians have to employ it, and one which is peculiarly acceptable to God ; but that there are *other* ways in which they may be " kindly affectioned one toward another," and in which, though their hands may be filled with no pecuniary offering, the words that breathe, the thoughts that burn, the feet that run on errands of love, shall all be precious in the sight of God, and emit a perfume fragrant as incense.

In the second place, it is to be constantly recollected that the external act, the thing done, the money expended—however large its amount, or diversified its application—is all utterly worthless unless it be the expression of an inward principle. Christian obedience must be the offspring and result of Christian faith; it must flow from the fountain of love,—of love to God and man. Without this, the most laborious work can have in it nothing of the nature of Christian service ; the most splendid donations will be no " sacrifice." Instead of being " acceptable " as sanctified virtue, they may be frowned upon and rejected as splendid sins. " Though I speak with the tongues of men and of angels, and have not charity, I am become as sounding brass, or a tinkling cymbal. And though I have the gift of prophecy, and understand all mysteries and all knowledge; and though I have all faith so that I could remove mountains, and have not charity, I am nothing. And *though I bestow all my goods to feed the poor*, and though I give my body to be burnt, and have not charity, it profiteth me nothing."* In this striking way does St. Paul set before us the utter worthlessness of everything of the nature of outward service—beneficent deeds, in the form of the liberal bestowment of property, among other things—separate from the exercise of that love, which is the fruit of faith and the gift of the Spirit. The language he employs no more condemns the giving of money " to feed the poor " than it condemns the exercise of persuasive speech, the exposition of prophecy, or the inculcation of dogmatic truth. It rather assumes that all are to be attended to—the mental and spiritual gifts exercised, and pecuniary donations freely made—but that neither the one nor the other can be a service to God, or acceptable to Him, if unconnected with an inward divine life,—with spiritual and earnest love.

In the third place, it is to be noticed, that, while without this love, the most liberal benefactions sink

* 1 Cor. xiii. 1—3.

into insignificance and go for nothing, *with* it the smallest contributions, the least possible gift or service, rises into a sacrifice, and is esteemed worthy of the divine regard. The acceptableness with God of what is done for Him, is not regulated by the magnitude of the work, but by the spirit and principle from which it springs. The widow's mite, tremblingly dropped into the treasury,—the cup of cold water given to a disciple in the name of a disciple,—the whispered word or the sympathetic tear of one who has neither gold nor silver to offer—these things, small in themselves, become large and valuable when prompted by love. "If there be first a willing mind, it is accepted, according to that a man hath, and not according to that he hath not." * Great and little, large and small, as applied by us to the material or amount of outward service,—are not the measure of that service in the divine estimation. "God seeth not as man seeth." He judges not by "outward appearance," but by the condition and actings of the heart, and with HIM "*love is the fulfilling of the law.*"

In the fourth place, it is to be remembered, that for beneficent acts, in the form of pecuniary liberality, to be "a sacrifice, acceptable, well pleasing to God," the man must be blameless in respect to the discharge of previous obligations. Christian beneficence must

* 2 Cor. viii. 12.

be wise and prudent, consistent and just. "God hates robbery for burnt-offering." He would not accept, in ancient times, bullocks or rams, oil or incense, offered by those who defrauded the widow, or oppressed the poor. Nor would He, we may be certain, have looked with pleasure on any alms or contributions given by such,—who, while dropping their gifts from one hand, were keeping back with the other what was justly due to those they were defrauding. In the same way, there are relative claims which are first to be met, before the way is open for public benefactions. Our Lord condemned the hypocrisy of the Pharisees, and stigmatized their teaching as immoral and odious, because they said that if a man's parents—his "father and mother"—needed his help, it was a sufficient reason for his refusing to assist them, if he could say that he had devoted his money as an offering to the temple, and must needs keep it that he might give it to God!* As if God could accept a voluntary gift which was obtained by the neglect of a standing obligation. In the same spirit the apostle teaches, that those who had aged or poor relations were to contribute to their support, and thus "to show piety at home," and not to let "the church be charged."† Paul would rather have had a man do that, though he gave nothing to a collection, than not do it and give largely. In the

* Mark vii. 10—13.   † 1 Tim. v. 3, 16.

same way, debts must be paid—every obligation and liability discharged—before a gift to others can be a sacrifice to God. If a man were to build a church, or restore a cathedral,—or endow either,—and to neglect the payment of his debts,—his professed beneficence would be an abomination. So true is it, in every sense, that outward acts must be regulated by principle; and that pious benefactions, to *be* pious, must be sanctioned by justice as well as prompted by love.

It seemed well to us, instead of advancing to-day to our third proposition, to interpose here these few explanatory and modifying remarks. In everything there is a danger of becoming one-sided. In benevolent acts, thoughtfulness and wisdom are quite as necessary as feeling and sentiment. Actual obligations never clash, though sometimes it may be difficult to determine which is first to be obeyed. In the present case, the line of duty is *theoretically* clear; the danger is, of men not seeing it from interest or selfishness on one side or the other. We have constant need of the purifying influences of the Holy Spirit, to enable us first to *see* what is right, and then to dispose us firmly to follow it;—not insensible to, but not governed by, human opinion;—always seeking to do that, in doing which—giving or withholding, or giving in one way and not in another— we may alike be " acceptable, well pleasing to God."

Sermon IX.

Luke xvi. 9.

"Make to yourselves friends of the Mammon of unrighteousness; that, when ye fail, they may receive you into everlasting habitations."

IN collecting and arranging the New Testament statements as to the matter in hand—namely—"that money may be put, religiously and benevolently, to a good use,"—we suggested that the best thing we could do would be, to set the evidence before you in a series of connected propositions;—each proposition being sustained by Scripture proofs;—the whole to be so disposed as to lead to some distinct and definite conclusion.

In the prosecution of this plan, we have had brought under review the first two links of the chain;—in other words, the first two propositions of the series have been exhibited and sustained. After simply *re*-stating these, and thus recalling them to your minds, we shall advance to those which remain to be adduced.

The first proposition was this:—"That the pious

and benevolent employment of money—the giving of the money itself, or of what money represents—in the way of kind and beneficent deeds, is *one of the required forms of Christian obedience.*"

The second proposition was,—" That this duty—this required form of religious obedience—is represented in the New Testament as something which, when properly rendered, *is peculiarly acceptable and pleasing to God.*"

The third proposition, which we are now to introduce and to proceed to substantiate, is this :—" That *this beneficent use of money,* which is first *required as obedience,* and then represented *as peculiarly acceptable,* is further represented (after having been received and accepted) AS BEING HELD BY GOD IN SPECIAL REMEMBRANCE.

Beneficent acts, right in spirit and principle, though they may be forgotten by the *doer*—who may not let his "left hand know what his right hand doeth "—are not forgotten by Him to whose will they have an ultimate respect, and by whom they are received as a sacrifice. They have a relation to God, and are regarded by Him, long after they have been accomplished and have passed away from the memory of men. They do not terminate with their being finished and done with here, or—so to speak—with the immediate pleasurable impression on the Divine

Mind. That impression is retained and prolonged. He, to whom they rise up as incense, gives to them, as it were, a substantial embodiment in the upper world;—lays them up there as valuable treasure belonging to His children;—and thinks of and surveys them with satisfaction and complacency.

The one idea at present before us, of God's special *remembrance* of beneficent deeds, is of course involved in those passages which connect them with men's having "treasure in heaven," and "being rich towards God," to which we have just made a passing allusion,—and which will be referred to presently as implying or expressing something more,—but it is to be found standing out by itself, distinctly and vividly enunciated, in one or two memorable statements. Take *two*. The first referring to an individual; the second, to a community.

I.

You remember the interesting sketch of Cornelius, in the tenth chapter of the Acts of the Apostles. "He was a devout man; one that feared God with all his house; *who gave much alms to the people; and who prayed to God alway.*" He set apart, as you may see by carefully weighing all the incidents of the story,—he set apart a day for special fasting and prayer. After being so engaged—from an early hour, we should imagine, till three o'clock in the afternoon—"he saw, in a vision, evidently, an angel of the Lord coming in to him, and saying, 'Cornelius!'" The angel had a special message to deliver, with which we have nothing at present to do; but he *introduced* that message by a preparatory statement which remarkably illustrates our present proposition. "Cornelius! *thine alms have come up for a memorial before God.*"* Such is the report of the historian. As repeated afterwards to the Apostle Peter by Cornelius himself, the words are—"thine alms *are had in remembrance* in the sight of God." † The sense is the same, while the difference of phraseology is just enough to tinge the idea with a diversity of colouring, and to fix it in the imagination as well as in the memory.

In the one case, there is a picture on which the eye of the mind looks. The alms of Cornelius rise up to heaven. They are laid down, like precious stones, on the sacred pavement. One after another, and in quick succession, additions are made, till the mass rises and becomes a monument,—a sign in heaven, conspicuous and significant, bearing witness to its inhabitants there, of what has been done and is doing on earth; a memorial, too, not only to *them*, but to "Him," also, "that sitteth upon the throne," —for they are a memorial " before God ; "—they are

* Acts x. 4. † Ver. 31.

so placed that He may see them,—that His eye may rest continually upon them,—that they may be kept in mind, as it were, and not suffered to be forgotten; —just as we have in the Prophets the strong figurative language respecting the Church, that God could not forget her, because He had set her "in the light of His countenance," and "had engraved her name on the palms of His hands." "Cornelius, thine alms have come up *as a memorial* before God."

In the other statement, "thine alms are had in remembrance in the sight of God," there is the same idea; but the *outer*, or objective portion, if we may so speak, is subordinate. Here, it is not so much for the imagination to picture the figure of a visible memorial, as for the reason to realize the spontaneous action of the Divine Mind. It is God, actively and purposely, as it were, recalling, and thinking about, and dwelling upon the thought of the beneficent deeds of his servant Cornelius. The alms of the man have come up, and been accepted, and accepted with complacency;—but more than that, they are recollected by God, and are constantly had " by Him *in special remembrance.*"

What gives to this fact a singular suggestiveness is the circumstance, that Cornelius was neither a Jew nor a Christian; he was not even a proselyte, properly speaking. He was simply a Gentile; a Roman by birth, and one who had been an idolater by religion.

But he was a man of deep and earnest thought; by study and prayer he had worked his way to the reception of the pure theism of the Hebrew creed, though he had not connected himself with the Hebrew Church. He was now in a state of further enquiry, and was anxious to understand what was the meaning of the popular rumour, and what its import to *him*, respecting a Messiah who was said to have appeared in the person of Jesus. Such was the man; a man of no church,—not a Jew, and not a Christian as yet; but a conscientious, earnest, devout man,—just and upright, charitable and beneficent,— at once "seeking after God, if haply he might find Him," and "doing His will" as far as he knew it. Of such an one is the record we have received. *To* him, the testimony is borne from heaven, that "his alms have gone up thither as a memorial;"—*From* him is to be learnt on earth, even by an Apostle, that " God is no respecter of persons," but that " in every nation, he who feareth God and worketh righteousness is accepted of Him."

The other passage to be referred to in proof of the position we are now maintaining—the Divine *remembrance* of beneficent acts—has respect to a number of persons, and not merely to an individual. It occurs in the sixth chapter of the Epistle to the Hebrews, and is to this effect:—"*God is not unrighteous to forget* your work and labour of love, which ye have shewed toward His name, *in that ye have ministered to the saints and do minister.*"* In the context, the Apostle is drawing a parallel between unfruitful Christians and barren and unproductive land. "The earth which drinketh in the rain that cometh oft upon it, and bringeth forth herbs meet for them by whom it is dressed, receiveth blessing of God; but that which beareth thorns and briars is rejected and is nigh unto cursing; whose end is to be burned." Without saying that he meant this by way of analogy—an illustration of spiritual things by natural—the writer assumes that his intention is so obvious as not to be mistaken, and he therefore immediately carries on the thought by applying it with a plain, literal directness, to the Christian people to whom he writes. "But, beloved, we are persuaded better things of you, though we thus speak."—"Better things of you;" that is, not barrenness and sterility, but fruit; the fruit of *visible Christian goodness,*—and that in some degree corresponding to the heavenly influences which, like rain and dew, had descended upon them. And he finds these in their "work" and "labour;"—not only in their Christian services generally, as the "work of faith," but in their "*labour of love;*"—in their earnest and energetic affection, which had manifested itself in positive acts;—these acts consisting, among

* Heb. vi 10.

other things, of pecuniary beneficence. "They had ministered to the saints;"—that is, ministered *to their necessities* by contributions of money, or of money's worth. They had done this, and they had done it out of regard to the Divine Name; for in doing it to God's saints, they had done it to *Him*, by whose Name they were called and known. And these acts it was—these loving and beneficent deeds—which, it is solemnly affirmed, "God does not forget." Nay, the thought is put in a form which we had not dared to use, if we had not got for it the highest authority. It is said,—"God *is not unrighteous*" to *forget* "work and labour" expended thus! As if, should he do so, an imputation might rest on His justice and rectitude. This is strong language, but it is not ours. It fell from an Apostolic pen; was approved and sanctioned, if not immediately suggested, by the Spirit. You see it in the Book; and what you read there, it cannot be wrong for ministers to repeat, though it certainly *would* be wrong for people to find fault with them because they do.

On all matters, especially on those which relate to faith and obedience, we regard the Book as speaking with authority. It comes to us as law. The "holy writings" are "given by inspiration of God," and are "profitable for doctrine, for reproof, for instruction in righteousness, that the man of God may be perfect, thoroughly furnished unto all good works." So long, then, as we simply set before you Scriptural truth in Scriptural language,—giving the Divine thought, "not in the words which man's wisdom teacheth, but in those which the Holy Ghost teacheth,"—we set forth that which is at once true and imperative; that which is not to be disputed but believed. This, and nothing but this, we are attempting to do in the whole of this argument. We have cited texts, and have so sought to explore and explain them, as to get at their plain, literal, and *intended* sense. In the prosecution of our purpose, we have fairly made out, we think, the three things hitherto exhibited;—first, —that beneficence is a duty;—second,—that it is one which is specially acceptable, well-pleasing to God;— and thirdly,—that those loving acts in which it consists (pecuniary gifts among them) constitute a memorial in heaven of what good men do upon earth; they are by God Himself " had in remembrance;"— nay, He is "not unrighteous," or unjust, "to forget them." We take all these statements to mean what they say. Such is plainly the prescribed duty;— such the revealed facts respecting it when properly discharged. From the last of these facts,—and from the striking manner in which it is conveyed to us,— the inference seems obvious, that God *must have some end to answer,*—some *definite purpose,* some *ultimate object,—with a view to which,* He is so intent on remembering, so unwilling to forget, those offerings and sacrifices with which He is "well-pleased."—Our next proposition will lead to the examination of this question.

II.

We are now brought to the fourth and *last* proposition which we have to present to you. It is this:—" That *that* Christian beneficence, which, in itself, is binding as a duty,—when rendered, acceptable as a sacrifice;—when accepted, remembered as a memorial;—is further represented *as productive, to those who exercise it, of many and varied beneficial results;* in other words,—and in words at once plainer and more Scriptural,—*beneficent acts are followed by reward.*"

We are well aware that there is a great dread among some people of any approach to such a word as "reward." They think it militates against the freedom and graciousness of the Gospel, and is inconsistent with the fact that human obedience must always be so imperfect that man, do what he may, can *deserve* nothing. For the sake of those who thus feel, and may thus object, it may be as well here to interpose a remark on the subject generally—(the Christian doctrine of reward)—before looking at the passages which connect it with the matter immediately before us.

III.

It is to be observed, then, that whatever any one may think or say, the idea of "reward," somehow or other, pervades the New Testament. The word is continually turning up. It is used in relation to what is to be bestowed in the future world, and to what may be received and enjoyed in this. It is of no use shutting our eyes to this fact. What we have to do is, not to deny what is so obvious, but to endeavour to understand what it really means. It must have *some* meaning, or the word would not be there; it must have some *great* meaning and some great object, for, being where it is, it is a word authorized by God himself, employed at His suggestion, and employed in the most solemn manner for instruction and encouragement. It is employed, you will find, to stimulate obedience and enlarge hope; to comfort and cheer under trial and loss; to reprove the indolent,—to recall the wandering,—and to confirm the loyal in the service of righteousness.

Just recollect some of the passages in which the idea of *reward* is not only implied, but explicitly declared. One of the most impressive representations of the Divine character is in these words;—"he that cometh unto God must believe that He is, *and that He is a rewarder of them that diligently seek Him.*"

* Heb. xi. 6.

Then, the word was constantly falling from the lips of our Lord. It occurred in His announcements of truth and duty; it was heard when He predicted the future coming of the Son of Man; it was pronounced from heaven in the visions of the Apocalypse, and in the hearing of John, among the last utterances of the glorified Christ with which the volume of revelation is closed.

Some of the Lord's teaching was to this effect;— "Rejoice and be exceeding glad, for *great is your reward in heaven.*"* "Your heavenly Father *will reward you openly.*"† To one He promised a "*prophet's* reward;" to another, "*a righteous man's* reward."‡ To some He gave the encouragement— "verily I say unto you," such an one "*shall in no wise lose his reward;*"§ others He exhorted in this way,—"do good"—love and lend—"*and your reward shall be great.*"‖ In predicting the future He said, "The Son of man shall come in the glory of His Father with His angels; and *then He shall reward every man according to his works.*"¶

One who heard the word as it was thus spoken on earth, heard it afterwards as it was uttered from heaven, and uttered in a manner the most solemn and impressive:—"I am Alpha and Omega, the beginning and the end, the first and the last. And

* Math. v. 12. † Math. vi. 4—6. ‡ Math. x 41.
§ Math. x. 42. ‖ Luke vi. 35. ¶ Math. xvi 27.

behold, I come quickly; and *my reward is with me, to give to every man according as his work shall be.*"*

In the writings of the most distinguished of the Apostles, Paul and John, we have the idea set forth in various aspects and in different relations. The following passages will substantiate this statement. "Every man *shall receive his own reward.*"†
"The fire shall try every man's work of what sort it is. If a man's work be burnt, he shall suffer loss; *if a man's work abide, he shall receive a reward.*"‡ "*Let no man beguile you of your reward.*"§ "Whatsoever ye do, do it heartily, as to the Lord; knowing that *of the Lord ye shall receive the reward* of the inheritance."‖ "Cast not away your confidence, *which hath great recompense of reward.*"¶ "Moses had respect *to the recompense of the reward.*"**
"Look to yourselves that ye lose not those things that ye have wrought, but that *ye receive a full reward.*" ††

Now with all this scriptural evidence—this constant repetition of the idea of reward, this putting it forth under all aspects and for all sorts of purposes—it is useless to attempt to deny or to disguise the fact, that there *is* and *must* be a Christian doctrine of

* Rev. xxii. 12. † 1 Cor. iii. 8. ‡ 1 Cor. iii. 14.
§ Col. ii. 18. ‖ Col. iii. 24. ¶ Heb. x. 35.
** Heb. xi. 26. †† 2 John ver. 8.

reward *of some sort or other.* The proof that the thing is there, ("in the volume of the Book"), is ample and demonstrative; *what* the thing itself *is,* that is the point that is to be determined.

All that we deem it necessary to say at present is this:—the Christian doctrine of reward has nothing to do with the pardon of sin, or the justification of the sinner. Man, as man, burdened with guilt and amenable to law, cannot be saved by his own works and deservings. *Mercy* and *salvation* are to be accepted as the gift of God, through Jesus Christ. Work and reward are here out of the question. It is different, however, with those works *which are the fruit of faith,* and which constitute the obedience of a Christian man. These, though always imperfect, and never entitled to a reward of merit, are yet represented as being followed by what may be called a reward of congruity. That is to say, partly by way of natural consequence, and partly by the way of gracious bestowment, the acts and habits of Christian obedience are hereafter to be followed by results, which, in measure or degree of glory and blessedness, shall bear a correspondence to what was actually attained to here. In other words, the Divine principle in man, according to its present culture and development, will be followed hereafter by *that for which it is fitted;*—this fitness—the reality and degree of that development and culture out of which it springs and in which it consists—being ascertained and proved by the penury or the richness of the fruits of faith—the nature and number of the actings of love—in every individual.

Such, in general terms, is the Christian doctrine of future reward. Properly understood, it is neither inconsistent with justification by faith, nor can it be productive of anything like selfish and sordid calculation. The more deeply we ponder, and the more earnestly we desire " the recompense of reward," the more shall we be anxious to increase and abound "in all holy conversation and godliness." The rewards of Eternity cannot in their nature be anything external. The words of our Lord, which both instructed and rebuked the two ambitious disciples, express, not so much the limitation of power, as the law of congruity;—" to sit on my right hand and my left is not mine to give, *except* to them for whom it is prepared,"—those, of course, who are prepared for *it*. Whatever the glory may be, or the measure or degree of it, which shall constitute the reward of the saved in the world of light, it will be something that will follow, as by appropriate sequence, *the previous spiritual condition of their minds.* The same law will rule in heaven that we recognise here,—the law that makes it *impossible to enjoy* any conferred or conspicuous honour, that does not harmonize with our internal consciousness. Nothing is so painful as approbation or reward secretly felt to be undeserved or inappropriate. Apply this to spiritual things. Justification by faith—gratuitous forgiveness, with whatever that of itself involves—can be gladly and gratefully accepted by *the sinful,* because given to and received by them *as such.* But to be hailed and welcomed by a "well done, *good and faithful* servant," would be felt to be a mockery, if "fidelity" and "goodness" had not *previously* been cultivated and displayed. To any one burdened by an opposite consciousness, crowns and kingdoms could give no pleasure—*none,* even if offered to be bestowed by Christ—*if the ground and reason* on which they were *publicly declared* to be conferred, was *felt* to be something which did not exist, and had never been. It is in this way that the Christian doctrine of reward is seen to be spiritually animating and practical. If any man wish for the distinctions of heaven, that wish can only be gratified by his being *now*—in purpose, at least, and sincere effort—*that* which he is anxious to be on high. He who is "to shine as the brightness of the firmament" in the future world, must, in the present life, by essential holiness, be "a partaker of the glory that is then to be revealed." This being understood, low motives and calculating expediency are out of the question. The desire for the reward becomes one and the same with love for the service. Such a desire will never contravene doctrinal Christianity, nor corrupt the source or sully the purity of practical obedience.

We have thought it well to give at once this general explanation. It is of necessity imperfect, but imperfect as it is, if we keep it in mind, we shall be the better prepared for listening to the argument of our next discourse, which, as we have intimated, will be to show, that "accepted and remembered acts of beneficence are capable of, and are to be followed by, reward."

˚ A part of the last two pages is transferred from a dis course of the author's in which the subject referred to is discussed. It is entitled " Salvation by Fire and Salvation in Fulness," and is contained in "Tower Church Sermons," a small volume published in 1851.

Sermon X.

MATH. x. 41, 42.

"He that receiveth a prophet in the name of a prophet, shall receive a prophet's reward; and he that receiveth a righteous man in the name of a righteous man, shall receive a righteous man's reward. And whosoever shall give to drink unto one of these little ones a cup of cold water only in the name of a disciple, verily I say unto you, he shall in no wise lose his reward."

THE statement to be illustrated, in this second part of our general argument, was, as you are aware, this :—" that money may be put to a good use."

The *sort of use* intended, was, you will remember, explained to be,—not its wise and prudent secular employment, but its employment religiously, or for benevolent and philanthropic purposes.

The *good* belonging to or springing out of this use of money, was to be understood, it was said, as comprehending good, in the sense of beneficial result, not only to those to whom, or for whose advantage, the money was given, but (as suggested by the text of the previous discourses*) to those who gave it,—to the

* Luke xvi. 9.

agents who planned and exercised the liberality. What they parted with, in a proper spirit and under hallowed influences, was to be expected to return to them *in some form or other of good to themselves.*

In proof and illustration of these general and comprehensive statements, we lay down the following series of connected propositions:—

First:—That the pious and benevolent employment of money—the giving of the money itself, or of that which money represents—is one of the required forms of Christian obedience.

Second:—That this duty—this required form of Christian obedience—is represented in the New Testament as something which, when properly rendered, is peculiarly acceptable and pleasing to God.

Third:—That this beneficent use of money, which is first required as obedience, and then represented as peculiarly acceptable,—is further represented, after having been received and accepted, as being held by God in special remembrance.

Fourth:—that that Christian beneficence, which, in itself, is binding as a duty;—when rendered, acceptable as sacrifice;—when accepted, remembered as a memorial;—is still further represented as productive, to those who exercise it, of many and varied beneficial results;—in other words, that kind and beneficent acts are followed by reward.

Of these propositions, the first three have been

fully and amply illustrated. Each of them has been sustained by the positive testimony of the New Testament, which with us is regal and authoritative, and from which there is no appeal. The evidence in support of the *last* of the series we have now to collect, arrange, and exhibit :—" Christian beneficence, kind and loving acts, *are followed by reward*."

We closed our last discourse with a brief exposition of the Christian doctrine of reward. We did this to meet a latent preliminary objection which undoubtedly exists in many minds, and to clear the subject of certain misconceptions which confuse and obscure it. It is our business now to proceed at once to the proof that the New Testament attaches reward, in various ways, to the exercise of that particular virtue which is the subject of our present argument.

I.

The first statement we make is this ;—that there are some passages which simply suggest the idea of reward—its possibility or certainty—without going into anything specific or particular. Of this class the following are illustrations. " Take heed that ye do not your alms before men, to be seen of them : *otherwise* (or if ye do so) *ye have no reward* of your

Father which is in heaven."* This, you observe, is a conditional statement. If you do so and so, "you have no reward of your Father," which of course involves, by necessary implication, the corresponding statement, namely, that if you act differently you *have* a reward, or shall have it, one time or other. But this idea, which at first is only *implied* and hinted at, is afterwards brought out into perfect distinctness, and is fully and positively expressed and declared. "But"—in opposition, that is, to the negative form of both precept and promise—"but, when thou doest alms, let not thy left hand know what thy right hand doeth; that thine alms may be in secret; and thy Father, which seeth in secret, *himself shall reward thee openly.*" The general idea is thus put by our Lord in two forms, so that we can neither mistake or evade it. On the one supposition, there is no reward; on the other supposition, a reward is certain,—"thy Father shall reward thee." It is not left to be deduced as an inference, but is made the subject of a distinct and positive declaration.

The same idea is involved in other of our Lord's divine sayings. Thus, "Lay not up for yourselves treasures upon earth, where moth and rust doth corrupt, and where thieves break through and steal: but *lay up for yourselves treasures in heaven*, where neither moth nor rust doth corrupt—and where thieves

* Math. vi. 1.

do not break through nor steal."* "Sell that ye have, and give alms; provide yourselves bags which wax not old, *a treasure in the heavens that faileth not*, where no thief approacheth, nor moth corrupteth."† In this way—figurative indeed, but intensely significant—did our Lord set forth the truth which he would inculcate, namely, that just as by hoarding a man may lay up a material treasure upon earth, *so*, by the beneficent employment of wealth he may as really, and far more securely, lay up a spiritual treasure in heaven. What that treasure may be, what it may consist of, he does not say; but he positively asserts two things respecting it,—first, that it is a reality, something secured and reserved for the individual who has laid it up; and secondly, that the man has acquired and accumulated it, and hoarded it in heaven, through the action of loving and beneficent deeds upon earth.

The same general truth is contained in the address of Jesus to the young ruler, recorded by Matthew, Mark, and Luke:—"sell all that thou hast, and distribute unto the poor, *and thou shalt have treasure in heaven*."‡ 'Thou hast "large possessions;" thou art " very rich;" thou canst retain thy wealth, if thou pleasest, under the conditions belonging to this life, namely, that it may be injured or stolen, or, if not, that thou and it must one day part company. But, if thou wouldst be perfect—sublimed in character,

* Math. vi. 19. † Luke xii. 33. ‡ Luke xviii. 22.

P

and secured against uncertainty—put forth thy hand towards thy wealth ; let that hand be moved by religious faith and genuine feeling ; take hold of, break, separate into fragments thy colossal possessions; scatter and disperse them by beneficent deeds, by being "willing to distribute, ready to communicate ;"— and verily I say unto thee, that ever and in proportion as thy riches shall be diminished and disappear here as a material possession, they shall pass into a new and permanent form in the upper world ; they shall be changed into a treasure in heaven,—a treasure which shall be thine, and thine for ever, as certainly as that which you now have is yours.'

It is hardly necessary further to corroborate, by additional quotations, this general statement of the idea of reward. At any rate, it will be enough to read over again the verses which we have this morning selected as a text :—"He that receiveth a prophet—" that is, he that shows him hospitality, that takes him in, and does him a kindness—"he that receiveth a prophet in the name of a prophet, shall receive a prophet's reward : and he that receiveth a righteous man in the name of a righteous man, shall receive a righteous man's reward. And whosoever shall give to drink unto one of these little ones a cup of cold water only in the name of a disciple, verily I say unto you, he shall in no wise lose his reward." Whatever the word reward may mean, whatever the thing itself may be,—of which these passages say nothing specific,—there it is. There is something or other which can thus be described, and is thus to be conceived of. And so intent is our Lord on establishing its certainty, and asserting a connexion between it and the very smallest service, that he employs his highest and most amplified form of asseveration to that end:—" whosoever gives but a cup of cold water," "*verily I* say unto you, he shall *in no wise* lose his reward."

II.

From this general suggestion of the idea of reward, we advance to a second statement; namely, that the good to the individual—the beneficial issue of loving and liberal acts, which may constitute this reward— may be something to be enjoyed in the present life; and further, that this something may take two forms: it may be a providential return, in temporal blessings; or it may be a spiritual communication of what shall nourish and enrich the inner life. Sometimes both of these things may be combined, constituting, so to speak, a mixed or double benefit.

In the apostolic age, a course of Christian beneficence during years of activity, when the individual was possessed of sufficient means, was rewarded in advanced life, through the arrangements respecting the widows *who were to be employed and supported by* *the Church.* " Let not a widow be taken into the number under three score years old;—well reported of for good works;—*if she have lodged strangers, if she have washed the saints' feet, if she have relieved the afflicted,* if she have diligently followed every good work." * Here, you observe, is a church-law which recognises Christian kindness; humble, but loving and laborious hospitable attentions; and which attaches to them, should circumstances render it necessary, a corresponding temporal provision. In advanced age, and in solitary widowhood, — with strength diminished, and the means furnished by a husband gone,—one who had delighted in the acts and offices of kindness to God's servants, might not only be unable to continue them, but might herself stand in need of sympathy and help. Let these be given to her, says St. Paul. And let these be given in a way which shall save her feelings from any painful sense of obligation. Let her be received into the number of those who have to perform certain services for the church in relation to their own sex. (Services comparatively light, it might be, but delicate and important, required by the habits of Eastern society.) Let her become one of this class. She will thus receive a moderate maintenance, while she will feel that she does something for it; that she does not eat the bread of charity or idleness, but is active and en-

* 1 Tim. v. 9, 10.

gaged, and that, too, in a way which will harmonise with her feelings, and fall in with the principles and habits of her former life, her years of loving and laborious beneficence.

There is an allusion to a temporal reward, or a return in kind for acts of beneficence, in what St. Paul says both to the Corinthians and the Philippians. To the first he writes to urge them to liberality, in the prospect of a collection which was about to be made in the churches of Achaia; and he tells them, for their encouragement, that "God is able *to make all grace abound* to them; so that *they always having all-sufficiency in all things*, may abound unto every good work."* They are thus persuaded to give under the conviction that property thus devoted will be followed, through God's blessing, by such an increase as will enable them to be more liberal in their future donations. It is the old doctrine of the Hebrew Scriptures, and may be regarded as an established providential law:—" There is that scattereth, and yet increaseth; there is that withholdeth more than is meet, and it tendeth to poverty." Riches may be increased by a part of them being freely and philanthropically employed. Such dispersed and distributed portion becomes so much seed, which bears fruit after its kind. The Apostle recognises this law, in what he immediately adds in the form of a wish or prayer:

* 2 Cor. ix. 8.

—" Now he that ministereth seed to the sower, both minister bread for your food, and *multiply your seed sown and increase the fruits of your righteousness.*" Mark that expression,—"Multiply your seed sown;" —that is their pecuniary contributions to a good object, which God will account as so much seed, and to which he will give a pecuniary increase in his providential blessing on their temporal concerns. And just as the natural harvest, will, for the most part, be in proportion to seed sown, so says the Apostle in relation to what pertains to pecuniary beneficence, " he that soweth sparingly shall reap also sparingly; and he that soweth bountifully shall reap also bountifully."

In writing to the Philippians, Paul had not to exhort and persuade them to liberality, but to acknowledge gifts, and to return thanks for their generous care of and kindness to himself. " Ye have well done that ye did communicate with my affliction." " I have received of Epaphroditus the things which were sent from you." And then he adds,—recognising and believing in the law of providential and gracious reward to which we are referring,—" But my God shall *supply all your need*, according to his riches in glory by Christ Jesus."* What is particularly observable in these words is this,—that God may be expected to regulate the return of Christian benefi-

* Philip. iv. 19.

cence, even in the sphere of worldly and temporal things, not merely according to the law of natural increase in the process of vegetation, but according to the glorious riches, the ample and affluent generosity, which distinguishes the gracious constitution of things in Christ Jesus. Spiritual blessings are no doubt included in the statement, and were in the mind of the apostle when he employed these words; but spiritual blessings were not *exclusively* meant. "All their need," which God was to supply, had a primary reference to *that sort of need* in himself, which they met and supplied when by sending a substantial gift they "communicated with his affliction."

There is another thing in this epistle to the Philippians, which bears upon our present topic, though it may easily be passed over without being observed. It appears that Epaphroditus, who undertook the journey from Philippi to Rome, as the bearer of the benevolence of the Church, so suffered, either from anxiety, or over-fatigue, or from being exposed to some poisonous malaria, that he fell sick. He was prostrated by disease. But his sympathy with the object of his mission and the design of his friends was so sincere, and his desire to show his love to the apostle so intense, that, in spite of pain and weakness and weariness, he counted not his life dear unto himself, if he could only contribute something to the comfort of one who was " the prisoner of Jesus

Christ,"—"His ambassador in bonds." This was a loving and beneficent act of the highest sort. And the apostle not only records it to his honour, but exhorts his friends to mark and reward it, by the manner in which they received him on his return, and by the increase of social respect with which he was to be regarded. "For the work of Christ he was nigh unto death, not regarding his life, *that he might supply your lack of services toward me. Receive him, therefore,* in the Lord with all gladness; *and hold such in reputation.*" * It is one of the gratifying and beneficial issues of distinguished benevolence, of liberal, laborious, or self-sacrificing love, that a man is looked up to, is esteemed and honoured by his associates and contemporaries—is referred to as one who "adorns" the doctrine of Christ as well as professes it. Such a man goes through life crowned with the secret benedictions of those whom he benefits, and attended by the public respect and confidence of all who know him.

III.

In further illustration of temporal advantage flowing from the exercise of beneficence, it may not be out of place to refer to two of the New Testament miracles.

The one is connected with loving and charitable labour; the other with the liberal expenditure of

* Philip. ii. 25—29.

money. There can be no doubt that the character of Dorcas, so eminently distinguished for her care of the poor,* was what so endeared her to the Church at Joppa, that the members of it were emboldened to send to Peter, in the hope that he might restore her to her useful labours, as he was reported to have cured a paralytic at Lydda. The apostle came at the request of the deputation, and on his arrival they endeavoured to interest him in the case of their friend, and to move him to exert his influence on her behalf, by showing him " the garments which Dorcas had made while she was with them." The appeal touched the sympathies of the apostle, and led him to seek, by supplication and prayer, permission from God to put forth the miraculous gift with which he was endowed. He kneeled down; he prayed; and then, turning to the body, he said, in the strength of faith, "Dorcas, arise;"—and she arose and sat up, and returned again to her "works of faith" and her "labours of love."

The other case is that of the Centurion who came to Jesus and besought him to come and heal his servant. Like every man truly and greatly good, he was unconscious of his own goodness, and felt and declared himself to be utterly unworthy to receive Jesus under his roof. But his character was known and honoured in the neighbourhood;—he was

* Acts ix. 36—41.

possessed of wealth, and he had devoted some of it to the honour and service of the God of Abraham. The people, when he approached, remembered his beneficence, and, in the exercise of a simple and natural logic, they thought of it as a ground on which they might urge his appeal and commend him to the compassionate notice of the Saviour. They said unto Jesus, in support of his request, "Lord, he is worthy for whom thou shouldest do this, for he loveth our nation and *hath built us a synagogue.*"* The man received the blessing he sought. And though that blessing was connected with the exercise of his faith, that faith might have been facilitated by the habit of mind which prompted his beneficence;—and the public testimony borne to that beneficence, may have wrought with his faith, and led to the exertion of that power which rewarded *both* by the recovery of his servant.

IV.

We have thus established two things;—first, that there is such a thing as reward, distinctly spoken of, as connected with and following beneficent deeds,— the loving and liberal use of money; and secondly, that one of the forms of that reward, in the present life, may be a return in kind,—the divine blessing resting upon labour and making it productive, or by

* Luke vii. 5.

other methods of providential recompence. We have contented ourselves with simply exhibiting the Scriptural proofs of what we have asserted, as our present business is to *ascertain* the law, and nothing else. By-and-by it may be our duty to expound principles, and to show how one thing is modified by another;—how, in relation to the present case, for instance, that, while it may be true that benevolence has a present reward, the *thought of that* is neither to be the ground with us of our being benevolent, nor are we to forget that, as in other things obedience to one law may be followed by appropriate beneficial results, though it may not hinder the coming of the evils that may be incurred by the neglect of others,—so a man may enjoy a natural and providential advantage from his habits of beneficence, and yet may come short of the higher blessings of redemption and salvation from his neglect or transgression of those higher laws on which these depend. We waive however all these matters at present. There remain to be exhibited, in further illustration of the proposition before us, the scriptural proof of *spiritual* advantages accruing here from religious beneficence,—and then, in addition to this, that there are rewards "to be brought unto it, at the revelation of Jesus Christ." These topics, however, must now of necessity be left to be taken up in another discourse.

Sermon XI.

MATH. x. 41, 42.

" He that receiveth a prophet in the name of a prophet, shall receive a prophet's reward; and he that receiveth a righteous man in the name of a righteous man, shall receive a righteous man's reward. And whosoever shall give to drink unto one of these little ones a cup of cold water only in the name of a disciple, verily I say unto you, he shall in no wise lose his reward."

"THAT Christian beneficence, which, in itself, is binding as a duty;—when rendered, acceptable as sacrifice;—when accepted, remembered as a memorial:—is further represented as productive, to those who exercise it, of many and varied beneficial results;—in other words, *that kind and beneficent acts are followed by reward.*"

In our last discourse, we could only give *part* of the proof of this final proposition; we have now, therefore, to endeavour to complete it. The two points to which we directed attention were these:—First; That the idea of reward—its possibility or certainty—is often put very generally, without the speaker or writer expressing any thing specific; as in the statements, "your Heavenly Father *shall reward you* openly;" "a cup of cold water shall not lose *its reward.*" Second; That, when we descend to particulars, this reward is found to be something that may be enjoyed in the present life; and further, that it may take two forms:—It may be a providential return in kind, a blessing on temporal supplies; or it may be a spiritual communication of what shall nourish and enrich the inner life. Sometimes these two things may be combined, constituting a mixed or double benefit.

The first only of these specified particulars came before us in our last discourse. We shewed, by several illustrations and testimonies, how both Christ and his disciples taught the possibility and likelihood of God blessing a man in the very same way and in the same sphere of things in which by his beneficence he blessed others. "Give, and it shall be given unto you; good measure, pressed down, and shaken together, and running over, shall men give into your bosom. For with the same measure that ye mete withal it shall be measured to you again."*

The matter that now comes in order before us is the second of the things just mentioned, namely, that kind and loving deeds—the exercise of the principle and of the habit of beneficence—may be followed by a present reward in the form of *spiritual*

* Luke vi. 38.

communications;—in gracious bestowments which shall advance the growth and augment the blessedness of the inner life.

I.

In proof of this you may, in the first place, accept the general statement that all excellence of all kinds is increased and strengthened by exercise;—that no particular virtue can be cultivated without advantage to the rest:—and that thus the habit of beneficence, because of its being a good and right thing, must, by way of natural consequence, operate beneficially on all the other good and right things that go to make up the Christian character. By that good use of money which we have been advocating, we do not mean *the mere act* of giving it away,—but its being given with thought, with serious calculation of what a man has, what God claims, and how best the duties of his stewardship may be discharged;—that it be given as a religious act, as a moral obligation, in the exercise of faith, in connexion with prayer, under the guidance of judgment and with simplicity of aim. Even in cases where feeling and sympathy may be suddenly excited, and the hand is moved by instinct and impulse, principles and feelings of a religious nature, though not consciously thought of at the time, will, from the necessary habits of a spiritual man, give a colour and tone to such isolated acts as shall make them expressions of faith and love. Now, no man can do a really right and good thing without being the better for it. "In the keeping of His commandments there is great reward." Conscientious obedience is to the soul, what air and exercise and nourishing food are to the body. The particular virtue of Christian beneficence—a willingness and readiness to benefit others—is of course subject to the action of this general law. The culture of a loving disposition, the opening of the heart to sympathy, the generous impulse and the liberal resolve, all act kindly and healthfully on every faculty of the inner man. The judgment and conscience, the intellect and the heart, are all alike strengthened and purified. "A good man is satisfied from himself;"—not *with* himself, as if he had nothing to mourn over and lament; but from himself —from the sentiments and acts which he cherishes and achieves, and which, by necessary consequence, through God's gracious constitution of things, fill him with a tranquil and inward peace. The man who, from some loving act of liberality or sacrifice,— some employment of time, influence, or money to do good to others,—the man who from these things goes into his closet or to the sanctuary, to the reading of the Bible or the worship of the church, will find that for him there is light and joy, and comfort and strength, in all such engagements. He does not think of what he has been doing; he does not talk of it either to himself or to God—unless it be to lament his deficiencies; but he cannot help its diffusing throughout his whole being such a harmony with divine things as tends to make him in every respect stronger and better. This is the law of spiritual life; of its growth and development, in respect to the exercise of every virtue; and we claim, of course, for the one before us, the benefit of the arrangement which belongs to all. A narrow-hearted, selfish, close-fisted Christian (for argument's sake admitting the possibility of his being a spiritual man) must be stunted in his growth, cold, dark, destitute of joy, from the bad influence on his soul of his miserable selfishness. "The liberal soul shall be made fat;" —he shall be strong and hearty—of fair countenance and joyous demeanour—from constantly breathing a healthy air, and living and walking in the divine sunlight.

So much for the general law, on which it would be both easy and pleasant to dilate, and which we commend to you as a most animating and exhilirating subject of thought. We proceed to notice, more particularly, some of these good issues, moral and spiritual, flowing from the exercise of beneficence, which are specified or hinted at in various texts.

II.

"Be not forgetful to entertain strangers; *for thereby some have entertained angels unawares.*"* The virtue of hospitality was of great importance in ancient times. But it involved expense; it was not always tendered, therefore, without grudging, or with a cheerful aspect, and was sometimes flatly and rudely refused. The apostle *suggests a motive to encourage its exercise* involving a general principle of universal application. 'Receive the stranger,—*he may be an angel in disguise.* He may bring with him the atmosphere of heaven. With him conversing, you may come to forget trouble and care,—receive light and knowledge,—have difficulties removed, and doubts quenched, and devotion quickened,—and feel like the disciples when "their hearts burned within them" as the Lord "talked with them by the way!" And when the stranger departs, he may leave behind him a joy in the memory, and a peace in the soul, which shall not die. And all this you would have lost, not only if you had rudely shut the door in his face and refused to take him in, but if you had neglected to open it,—selfishly enjoying your own comforts, and forgetting that a brother might be in want of a bed. You are not to entertain strangers because all of them are angels; nor to be disappointed and angry if they don't happen to turn out what you expected. But you

* Heb. xiii. 2.

are to "exercise hospitality" "without grudging," simply because it is right and kind and acceptable to God so to do,—and it *may* happen that sometimes you will find "that you have received an angel unawares." Of course the more frequently you show kindness to the stranger, the greater will be your chance of being favoured with the company of an angelic visitant.' All this admits of a very obvious application to ourselves. Let us not be forgetful to do kind acts, as we have opportunity; we shall often find that we get in return—and often in direct religious benefit—from those we assist, far more than what we give.

'"Give alms of such things as ye have, *and behold all things are clean unto you.*" * Our Lord spake this to some who marvelled that he did not wash his hands, as a religious ceremony, before he sat down to meat. They thought it was thus that men were to prepare themselves for touching food, if they were to avoid contracting uncleanness. 'I can teach you,' said our Lord, ' "a more excellent way." Cultivate the spiritual and moral affections; rise into a higher region than that of a superstitious and scrupulous ritualism; Especially open the heart to broad, healthy, benevolent sympathies; prove this by acts of positive beneficence;—and then, when you have thus cleansed and purified your souls by washing out

* Luke xi. 41.

of them the filth and stains of selfishness, you may sit down and eat without caring about washing your hands. "All things will be clean to you" because you yourselves will be clean. Ceremonial niceties will not trouble a soul that is strong and healthy from a heart pulsating with an earnest and fruitful love. God will accept your gift. He loves mercy far better than either ceremony or sacrifice. Give alms, do good, love your neighbour, honour God with your substance, and then "you may eat your bread with cheerfulness, and drink your wine, with a merry heart," whether you have poured water over your hands or not!' The lesson taught here is, that the culture of the benevolent affections, the wise and thoughtful exercise of a liberal beneficence, will strengthen the inner man, give tone and vigour to the religious character, raise it above the scruples and apprehensions of superstition, and save it from falling into formalism and hypocrisy.

"*If thou wilt be perfect*, go and sell that thou hast, and give to the poor, and come and follow me."[*] This was said to the young man who had kept all the commandments from his youth; who was moral and virtuous, and religiously disposed: who wished to know how he might inherit eternal life, and whom our Lord loved when he looked upon him, observing and acknowledging his sincerity and ingenuousness.

[*] Math. xix. 21.

He had done well in the lower sphere of external duty;—in being pure and upright, just and devout, according to the commandments. But there was a higher sphere into which he might enter; another life he might learn to live; and, "if he would be perfect,"—if he would have the deeper powers of his soul called out, and the nobler capacities of his spirit developed,—he must rise to the height of this diviner life. And the way to this, was through the exercise of a benevolence which should amount to *self-sacrifice* for the benefit of others. To sell all that he had, and to give to the poor, and to follow Christ, would advance or help him towards spiritual perfection. He could not follow Christ with all his heart, and be entirely conformed to him and satisfied with his service, unless he sold and gave away all that he had. If he did that, the earnestness that prompted, and the faith that lay at the bottom of the act, would be something within him to which "nothing would be impossible." The mere act of bestowing his fortune on the poor would not of itself have done much for him; but as, *in his case*, that fortune kept him from Christ, and came in between him and God,—if he got rid of it by an act of sacrifice, his soul would be free to rise towards heaven, as the balloon mounts upwards when the bags of sand are emptied out of it. The lesson here is, that there are *some cases* where acts of beneficence are religiously beneficial,—not so much by directly bringing down heavenly blessings, as by preventing men from setting their hearts on their possessions, loving and clinging to their wealth; by curing them therefore of this, or counteracting the tendency to it, and thus cutting the strings that would tie them to the earth.

"Blessed are the merciful, *for they shall obtain mercy.*" "*If ye forgive not* men their trespasses, *neither will your heavenly Father forgive ye, your trespasses.*" "Peter came to him and said, Lord, how often shall my brother sin against me, and I forgive him? till seven times? Jesus said unto him, I say not unto thee Until seven times; but Until seventy times seven."* And then, you remember, having said this, our Lord proceeded to illustrate his lesson by a parable founded on a money-transaction;—the benevolent remission of a large debt, and the cruel exaction of a small one. A servant owed his Lord 10,000 talents,—a sum which, however computed, would look immense in our language;—a fellow-servant owed *him* a hundred pence,—about three pounds. You know the story. How the Lord freely forgave the one; and how that one, after he had been forgiven, seized the other by the throat, and threw him into prison, on not immediately obtaining the paltry amount due to him; and how the Lord, indignant at such conduct, recalled to his presence

* Math. v. 7; vi. 15; xviii. 21, 22.

the selfish and cruel man, and not only reproved him, but revoked the act of forgiveness,—reimposed the debt,—and delivered him to the tormentors till he should pay it all. The parable is a comment on the beatitude—"blessed are the merciful, for they shall obtain mercy;" and on the conditional statement appended to the prayer taught to the disciples—"if ye forgive not men their trespasses, neither will your heavenly Father forgive you your trespasses." The three passages all refer to the spiritual advantages which may accrue to the individual from the exercise of a loving and merciful disposition; a disposition which may show itself in many ways, and amongst the rest, by pecuniary beneficence. "God is not unfaithful to forget this." Those who in any way have exercised mercy, and shown love, and hated the cruelty of rigid exaction, remembering how much they had in themselves to be forgiven,—without saying that this constitutes the ground and reason why God shows them mercy, or that they do those things to obtain that,—we do say, that such things *belong to that state of mind and heart*, which must be possessed if a man is either to pray aright for the forgiveness of his sins, or to be in a proper spiritual condition to receive it.

III.

We close this part of the argument, by referring to

the most striking and wonderful statement which the New Testament contains on the spiritual advantage to a Christian man of the habit of beneficence. We have had the passage before, or part of it, for other purposes; we take it again for the last and most suggestive use to which it can be applied. " Charge them that are rich in this world, that they be not high-minded, nor trust in uncertain riches ; that they do good, that they be rich in good works, ready to distribute, willing to communicate :—*Laying up in store for themselves a good foundation against the time to come, that they may lay hold on eternal life.*"* Such was the solemn charge which " Paul the aged," when drawing nigh to the close of his ministry, enjoined Timothy to lay on the heart and conscience of the church, and especially on the consciences of rich men. It is perfectly plain. It is sharp, and pointed, and far removed from mistiness or ambiguity. It is such a statement, as, if it had not been found in the New Testament, would have been resented by many if they had heard it from the lips of a modern minister. They would not only have accused him of " not preaching the Gospel," but of actually perverting it; nay, of using the very language in which its humbling and exclusive declarations are conveyed, for the apparent purpose of ministering to pride. ' What ! " a man to lay up *for himself* a good foundation." Why, " other

* 1 Tim. vi. 17—19.

foundation can no man lay than which *is laid*,—Jesus Christ." To lay up for himself "a good foundation," and that, too, by "being *rich in good works;*"—as if a sinner could be rich in anything:—one, who is "poor, and miserable, and blind, and naked," and whose best works are as "filthy rags!" A good foundation "against the time to come, that he may *lay hold on eternal life!*" Why, *Christ* is "the way, the truth, and *the life*." Christ must lay hold of *him*, if he is to be saved from sinking at his last hour! And as to any works he has "laid up in store," he must throw them away;—"what was gain to him must be counted loss for Christ." Rich and poor must alike come to this, for both must be saved in the same way.' It is easy to see how some people would have spoken thus, and have found fault with the preacher for "subverting the Gospel," if Paul had not written the words before us; and if, without his authority, any one of us had dared to use them. But there they stand. There is no getting over them. They must be perfectly evangelical, since they are unquestionably apostolic; and they must be well worthy of serious thought from the solemn manner in which they are introduced.

The fact is, there is no difficulty in harmonizing the passage with the Evangelical system properly understood. Man, as a sinner, when first met by the Gospel, and seeking to enter on the Christian life, and all the way through in habitually adverting to first principles, is to exercise faith in Christ as his only hope; to trust in him as the only foundation, and to accept forgiveness as a free gift. None of his works can be thought of for a moment, as the ground or reason of reconciliation. But, at the end of life, when, as a Christian professor, a son of God and not merely a child of Adam, he is going to give an account of his stewardship, then, if he is "to give in that account with joy, and not with grief,"—if he is "not to be ashamed" in the presence of his Lord, but to stand with humble confidence before him,—he must have the consciousness of diligence and fidelity, and be able to feel that he has not lived in the habitual neglect of such service as he was required to discharge. And if that service consisted especially *in the stewardship of wealth*,—if Christ entrusted him with large means and ample opportunities of using them for *Him*,—he will have no peace in his last hours, and be hardly able to look forward without terror, if he has been covetous, niggardly, grasping and selfish ; or if his acts of beneficence have been utterly disproportioned to what he possessed. The words of St. Paul have nothing to do with the acceptance of the sinner. They are concerned exclusively with the consciousness of the Christian, when the sphere of action is *lying behind him*, and the Lord, the Judge, is "standing at the door." It will not do then, for the rich man who has professed Christ for thirty or forty years, to think of going to him as a " poor sinner,"—having never done anything with all his money but spent it on himself or saved it for his children. If God's servants to whom he has given large possessions, are to lay hold on eternal life with a firm hand and undisturbed assurance, they must come to their end "like a shock of corn, fully ripe;" rich in good and beneficent deeds; having in themselves the tranquil consciousness that they have "dispersed abroad," "given to the poor," "communicated and distributed," with a loving heart and liberal hand; and that thus they were faithful in the use and employment of *that special talent* that was committed to their trust. In this way only, as St. Paul teaches us, can a rich Christian have comfort and peace "when heart and flesh faint and fail." As sinners, the foundation of our hope is the work of Christ; but as Christians, the confidence and joy which are to sustain us in the prospect of meeting the Lord, must be connected with the confidence of our having done the special work "which was given us to do." That work may have been acting or suffering; speaking or writing: the ministry or the deaconship; talents or genius; influence or power; —something or other additional to the ordinary duties and common obligations of every day life. But whatever it was, we must not be disturbed, when life is ebbing, with the terrible thought that our special talent has either been abused and misspent, or bound in a napkin and buried in the earth. And if that talent, as I have already said, happen to be wealth, woe to the rich Christian professor, who, instead of using it for God and man, has clutched at and kept it with a hard hand. It will crush him with its weight when he comes to die. It will be like thick clay on the wings of the soul, and will utterly prevent it from rising and soaring in gladness and joy to breathe the air of the upper world. Such a man may be saved;—but that will be all. He will not pass away in triumph and song; or if he does, *that* to survivors, who knew his inconsistency, may be more painful than if his sun had gone down in clouds and darkness.

IV.

In these several ways, does the New Testament distinctly teach how the exercise of beneficence may be attended with a reward in the present life; a reward of a directly spiritual nature, which contributes to the growth of the inward man,—his vigour and blessedness, his composure and peace as life advances, and his confident hope and tranquil triumph when the end comes, and he has to go forth to meet his Lord.

In addition to all that has been said, it may be recollected, that there runs through the New Testament this idea,—which will not be lightly thought of by any who value the intercessions of the faithful,— namely, that the loving and beneficent draw towards themselves the affectionate regards of those who are benefited by their deeds of kindness, and of those who witness their Christian liberality; and that, in their best moments, both remember them before God, giving thanks to Him for their work of faith and labour of love, and praying for their enjoyment of constantly continued and ever increasing donations of heavenly grace. You find Paul telling those who have done well, as good stewards of what they possessed, that in this way they may expect to be repaid. Moved and stimulated by the thought of their beneficence, he tells them how he himself remembers their good work in all his prayers, and how earnestly and constantly he supplicates God on their behalf.* It is not to be doubted that many a blessing descended on the souls of those for whom prayer was thus made continually. It is a blessed thing, depend upon it, to have the loving thoughts and the earnest intercessions of God's children,— especially of those who, though "poor in this world," are "rich in faith and heirs of the kingdom." That man is little to be envied, who, with large means, never does anything to make himself remembered or his name precious: and for whom no prayer is ever offered, no thanksgiving sent up to heaven. He, on

* Eph. i. 15, &c. Philip. i. 3—5. Col. i. 3, 4. 1 Thess. i. 2, 3.

the other hand, whose beneficence is conspicuous, or whose good deeds "cannot be hid," or, even if hid, are felt and remembered by those whom he benefits, will have many prayers rising continually to God on his behalf; and though his name and person may be unknown, the prayers will rise all the same to Him who will be felt to know who is intended; and blessings will be sought, and blessings secured, and they will be sure to descend on the soul and heart of the right man. "Scarcely for a righteous man will one die." The strictly just may have solid worth, but they do not excite and win love. "For a good man"—that is, *a liberal and benevolent man*, "some would even dare, or be ready to die."* They feel for him attachment, they glow with enthusiasm; and though they may not be called to die for him, they can pray for him, and they will do this, and he will be spiritually the better and the richer for such prayers, and he will know how to regard them as a most precious possession.

I must leave, I find, till next Sunday, the last link of the argument to be looked at,—*the anticipated rewards of the future life.* It may be possible, however, with that, to make some approach to the winding up of the whole matter, by adverting to some of those directions and lessons with which our discussion will appropriately close.

* Rom. v. 7.

Sermon XII.

LUKE XVI. 9.

"I say unto you, make to yourselves friends of the Mammon of unrighteousness, that when ye fail, they may receive you into everlasting habitations."

IN prosecuting our enquiry into the perils and advantages of wealth, through a series of discourses of which the present is the twelfth, we have often taken different texts, to indicate or foreshadow the different successive phases of the argument. This morning, we have to conclude the presentation of the Scriptural testimony on the subject, by setting before you the last link in the chain of thought we proposed to pursue, and, in doing so, we return to the text from which we started at first,—"Make to yourselves friends of the Mammon of unrighteousness, *that when ye fail, they may receive you into everlasting habitations.*"

These words, many of you will at once perceive, bear upon that particular topic which you will be expecting to hear discussed this morning, namely,—

"That Christian beneficence—kind and loving acts—are followed by reward."

What we have done, so far, in the establishment and illustration of this proposition, is this. We have shown, in the first place, that, in several New Testament statements, there is connected with the exercise of beneficence the general idea of reward, without any attempt to give it specificness by descending to particulars. Secondly, it has been shown that, when we descend to or look for particulars, we find that that which is meant by reward—the reward of loving and liberal deeds—may be something which can be enjoyed in the present life; and, further, that that something may take two forms,—it may be a providential return in kind, a blessing on men's temporal supplies; or it may be a spiritual communication, donations of gracious influence, to nourish and enrich the inner life. This second idea was the subject of our last discourse. *One thing yet remains* to complete the exhibition of Scriptural thought on the matter in hand, namely, that the New Testament teaches that all forms of loving service—every kind and degree of benevolent effort, and conscientious liberality—will be followed hereafter, in the arrangements of the future world, by such results as, to the good and faithful, shall be a direct, designed, and natural recompense.

This is what we have now to establish and illustrate,

and, with that, our general argument will have reached its close.

I.

In proceeding to develop the Scriptural proof of this final statement, we may begin with the more vague and general intimations, and gradually advance to the specific and precise. We remind you, then, in the first place, of those repeated sayings of our Lord, in which he lifts the thoughts and expectations of his hearers to the upper world, assuring them of the certainty that what they do to men, will be the means of their becoming "rich towards God." "Rejoice and be exceeding glad, for great is your reward *in heaven.*" "Sell all that ye have and give alms;—provide yourselves bags that wax not old, a treasure *in the heavens* that faileth not; where no thief approacheth, neither moth corrupteth." "Sell all that thou hast, and give to the poor,—and thou shalt have treasure *in heaven.*"* In these and similar passages the words "treasure" and "reward" are used interchangeably, as meaning the same thing. And this, as it is something which belongs to the individual, and is safely housed and laid up in heaven, must necessarily signify that it is kept and preserved for *him*, and that one day he should be put in possession of it. The very idea of laying up treasure,

* Math. v. 12. Luke xii. 33. Math. xix. 21.

implies that it is done with an object;—that at some future time it will come into use. And "treasure in heaven," whatever it may consist of, if it is to prove of any value, must either be ultimately brought to the man, or the man must be taken to it. It may as well rust, or rot, or be stolen by thieves, as bound up in bags, or locked in a safe, if it is never to be seen and enjoyed by its owner. Our Lord's words, therefore, in these memorable sayings, have no meaning, if they do not point to some future time—a future age, or a future world—when, what has now and here been laboriously accumulated, shall become a substantial and permanent possession.

This general idea, which so far is but a matter of inference, takes a positive form as to time and circumstance, in other of the suggestive sayings of the Master. "When thou makest a feast (a dinner or a supper) call not thy rich neighbours, lest they bid thee again, and a recompense be made thee; but call the poor, the maimed, the halt, the blind, for they cannot recompense thee, but thou shalt be recompensed *at the resurrection of the just.*"* There, you have something additional to what you had before. You have not only the laying up of the treasure, by the religious and beneficent use of worldly property; but you have the further idea of its being laid up for a future day, and of its being

* Luke xiv. 14.

positively realized in another and a new condition of things. You are to come into possession of it at "the resurrection of the just;" and still more, as it is to come in the form of "recompense," the language expresses not only the ultimate connexion between the present act and the future reward, but that that connexion is of such a nature as to amount to something like necessary consequence. The specific statement now before us may cast light on another of our Lord's previous and more general sayings;—"Let thine alms be in secret, and thy heavenly Father shall reward thee *openly*." This *might* refer to some immediate present blessing; some divine radiance, as it were, flowing from the inward satisfaction and peace that would fill the soul, which should shine forth before men, constraining so to speak their reverence and respect, and leading them to honour whom God had honoured. It might mean that;—but it might also mean—and looked at in the light of the subsequent statement we should take it to mean—that the time for God's rewarding "openly" what was done in secret, would be at "the resurrection of the just;"—in the presence alike of angels and men, when "the Son of man should come in his glory, and all nations be gathered before him."

II.

These two thoughts, found in our Lord's discourses in the Gospels,—the securing or laying up of something valuable in heaven by action upon earth, and the coming into possession of that at a future day,—these same thoughts are to be found in the Epistles, in their unerring expositions of the nature and prospects of the Christian life.

Properly to understand the teaching of St. Paul, you must always keep in mind the double aspect in which he presents the Christian dispensation :—that it to say, its aspect, primarily, to Humanity,—to men as men ;—and next its aspect to the Church,— or to men as recipients of the faith, and professedly members of the kingdom of God. In the first case, the Gospel is a message ; it is good news ; the proclamation of pardon ; the offer of free, unmerited, gratuitous salvation ; justification by faith ; reconciliation, acceptance, eternal life as " the gift of God through Jesus Christ." Such is the first aspect of the Gospel to the world and man. But, the Gospel being submitted to, and its privileges received, the Church becomes a kingdom, with a constitution and a law :—men, as Christian men, have services to fulfil, and obligations to obey, and responsibilities to meet,—a race to run, a warfare to accomplish, a stewardship to discharge,—and, in ultimate connexion with all this, there are crowns to be secured, and distinctions to be won in the future world, as the result of achievement and fidelity in this. The "*gift*" of God, through the redemption that is in Christ Jesus, is eternal life; but the "prize" of our high calling,—the elevation or splendour of individual position,—this is only to be obtained by earnestness and zeal, and exemplary devotion, in the course and the conflict which we pass through here. Hence, it may be quite possible, at the last day, for the sinner to be saved, but for the saint not to be crowned; for the *man* to be accepted in virtue of his faith, while the disciple and servant is unhonoured as the inevitable consequence of indolence or neglect. You will find this distinction running through the New Testament, necessarily underlying both its doctrinal statements and practical exhortations, and giving vividness and force to many of its expressions of personal feeling,—the Christian consciousness and inward experience of Apostolic men.

Keeping this distinction in view, and listening to a few passages from the Apostolic letters, you will see how they bear on our present object, which, so far, is only to prove that there is such a thing as a future reward to be secured through the activities of present obedience. The Apostle Paul, you all know, was the great advocate of gratuitous salvation. "By the grace of God" he was what he was. He had once gloried in the flesh, and thought himself rich in the works of a legal righteousness; but "what things were gain to him, he learned to count loss for Christ"; he threw them away as dross and refuse, esteeming them as nothing "for the excellency of the knowledge of Christ Jesus." Christ had taken hold of him, seized him, "apprehended" him, and thus, by a sovereign and gracious interposition, had snatched him from destruction and delivered him from death. So Paul felt as a man; so he believed and rejoiced as a sinner. But how did he feel as a *Christian* man? How did he teach others to feel? What were his notions of present duty, of pressing obligation, of surrounding peril, of the importance of faithfulness in the Master's service and of the connexion of all this with "the recompense of reward," which was to be given at last only to them by whom it should be won?—You have the answer in his own words; as you have also his description of his standing as a sinner justified by mercy. Recall both; put the last mentioned first, and thus place them in their natural order.

"By the works of the law shall no flesh living be justified." — "I through the law am dead to the law, that I might live unto God."—"I am crucified with Christ; nevertheless I live; yet not I, but Christ liveth in me; and the life which I now live in the flesh I live by the faith of the Son of God, who loved me, and gave himself for me."

"There is no condemnation to them that are in Christ Jesus." "Being justified by faith, we have peace with God."* So far we have *half* only of Paul's views, teaching, and experience. Now for the other half. "Not as though I had already attained, either were already perfect; but I follow after, if that I may apprehend that for which also I am apprehended of Christ Jesus." Christ, it would seem, seized on or apprehended him, and brought him from his wanderings; drew him, by an act of grace, into the right way; set him on his feet, opened his eyes, and then pointed to something in the far distance and said, "*Now*, fix your eye upon that;—as my servant, as one to whom I have given life, freedom, and facilities, lay hold upon, press toward, and manfully secure *that* object; *thus* realize and fulfil what was in my mind when I stretched out my hand, and laid hold of *you*." Paul was not disobedient to the heavenly vision. "Brethren, I count not myself to have apprehended—but this one thing I do, forgetting those things which are behind, and reaching forth unto those things which are before, *I press toward the mark for the prize of the high calling of God in Christ Jesus.*"† We have another illustration of this same feeling, in what he says in another letter. "Know ye not that they which run in a race, run all,

---

* Gal. ii. 16—20. Rom. viii. 1; v. 1.
† Philip. iii. 12—14.

but one obtaineth the prize? So run, that ye may obtain. And every man that striveth for the mastery is temperate in all things. Now they do it to obtain a corruptible crown; *we an incorruptible.* I therefore so run, not as uncertainly; so fight I, not as one that beateth the air : but I keep under my body, and bring it into subjection; lest that by any means, when I have preached to others, I myself should be a castaway." We have a more matured and a more confident development of this same sentiment, in the last letter that Paul ever wrote :—when the way had been trodden to which the Master had introduced him; *and the race and the battle were virtually concluded.* "Now I am ready to be offered, and the time of my departure is at hand : I have fought a good fight, I have finished my course; I have kept the faith; *henceforth* there is laid up for me a crown of righteousness, which the Lord, the righteous judge, shall give me at that day :"*—that is, at the day "of his appearing," what our Lord meant when he spoke of "the coming of the Son of man," and of "the resurrection of the just."

The same truth is illustrated by many other passages to which we might refer;—that is, the general truth that all faithful service,—zeal, earnestness, devotion, in working the work of God as

* 2 Tim. iv. 6—8.

Christian men,—shall be at last acknowledged and rewarded. This general truth, this broad and comprehensive statement, of course includes in it the recognition and recompense of every separate virtue; and, among the rest, of that virtue of beneficence with which our argument is concerned. We shall presently refer you to particular statements directly bearing on our special theme; but two or three more words on the general subject, in the form of Scriptural quotations, may not be amiss. " Every man's work shall be made manifest; for the day shall declare it, because it shall be revealed by fire; and the fire shall try every man's work of what sort it is. If any man's work abide, he shall receive a reward. If any man's work be burned, he shall suffer loss: but he himself shall be saved; yet so as by fire "* There you have the idea of a man being saved,—saved as a sinner on the ground of his recognized repentance and faith,—and yet, *as a Christian*, from some pervading unfaithfulness or defect, which though consistent with sincerity tarnished his character, losing his reward, and being exposed to shame rather than being honoured. Such a representation throws light on our Lord's words as spoken from heaven, and, in the Book of the Apocalypse, addressed to the churches,—to every member personally and individually. "Behold I come quickly;

* 1 Cor. iii. 13—15.

hold fast that which thou hast, that no man take thy crown." "Be thou faithful unto death, and I will give thee a crown of life."* The parables of the pounds and the talents illustrate the same general truth, — the connexion of present diligence and fidelity with future reward. The servant who remembered his Lord's will, felt his responsibility and did his work, gave in his account with joy; was not ashamed when he stood before Him, and received from his lips what was far more than a recompense for anything that he had either accomplished or endured. "Well done, good and faithful servant: thou hast been faithful over a few things, I will make thee ruler over many things; enter thou into the joy of thy Lord."† To enter into "the joy of the Lord"—into future fellowship with Christ, by participation of that which constitutes his reward—requires fellowship with him now, in his fidelity and devotion—his obedience and sufferings—his loyalty to God and benevolence to man. *He* could say, "I have finished the work which thou gavest me to do." "Greater love hath no man than this, that a man lay down his life for his friends." "The Son of man is come to seek and to save the lost, and to give his life a ransom for many." Christians cannot equal Christ in the perfection of his obedience, nor share with him in the nature of his sacrifice; but there is a

* Rev. iii. 11; ii. 10. † Math. xxv. 23.

principle that may pervade both action and suffering, and by this they may be fitted for "entering into his joy." "Wherefore, let us lay aside every weight, and the sin which doth so easily beset us, and let us run with patience the race which is set before us—looking unto Jesus the author and finisher of our faith; who, for the joy that was set before him, endured the cross, despising the shame, and is now set down at the right hand of the throne of God."* As perfect obedience and self-sacrificing love were crowned in the Master, so, in his servants, fidelity and beneficence, though imperfect and limited—but springing from faith, and earnest and sincere—shall be crowned too. The good and faithful shall be rewarded openly; publicly welcomed "into the joy of their Lord."

III.

These testimonies and reasonings would seem fully to establish the general truth, that by conscientious diligence, zeal, and fidelity in God's service, Christians lay up and secure to themselves a future reward. This being so, then, even if there were no texts to be adduced specifically referring to the reward of beneficence, the certainty of that reward would follow from the general truth by way of natural consequence. The greater includes the less. The whole is the

* Heb. xii. 1, 2.

aggregate of the several parts. A reward accorded to fidelity in all things, would involve the reward of each of the things that made up the all. What crowned therefore and beautified the whole family of the Christian virtues, would crown the individual members of the group. And as we have already proved that beneficent liberality—the faithful discharge of the stewardship of money—is one of the required forms of Christian obedience, that *it* would be rewarded amongst the rest, follows as a simple matter of course. This is further confirmed, as a logical inference, by what was also proved in former discourses,—that kind and loving acts, charitable and beneficent deeds, are represented as being peculiarly acceptable to God, and that, after being received, they are specially remembered, constituting a memorial in heaven of their agents upon earth. " God is not unrighteous to forget the work of faith and labour of love," of those who have " ministered to the necessities of the saints."—But such representations *imply* that this class of virtues stand out before the Divine eye with peculiar prominence, and could not therefore be overlooked in any reward confered upon the whole; and still further, that as the special remembrance of them must have some object,—as they must be kept in mind for some express purpose,—the likeliest thing is, that they are thus preserved, treasured up in the Divine memory, with a view to their being proclaimed and brought forth at last, and openly distinguished by distinct recognition and special reward.

There are some passages which almost seem to suggest (what, however, it will be heresy to mention,) that a thoroughly benevolent, and practically loving Christian man, will be less severely dealt with when called to his account, because of the consideration he has shown to others. "So speak ye, and so do," says St. James, " as they that shall be judged by the law of liberty;"* that is, by the Gospel, which is the law of love,—free, generous, brotherly love;—you are to be judged and tested by that. Speak and act thus, "*for* he shall have judgment without mercy, *who hath showed no mercy;* and mercy rejoiceth against judgment." This is but a comment on our Lord's words, "Blessed are the merciful, for they shall obtain mercy." With some feeling or expectation of this sort, it must have been, that St. Paul alluded to one who had done him a kindness when kindness was valuable to him, and spoke of him after this manner:—" The Lord give mercy to the house of Onesiphorus; for he oft refreshed me, and was not ashamed of my chain: but, when he was in Rome, he sought me out very diligently, and found me. The Lord grant unto him *that he may find mercy of the Lord in that day.*"† But without

* James ii. 12, 13.   † 2 Tim. i. 16—18.

dwelling upon these passages, which are thought by some of doubtful interpretation, we will close the whole argument, by referring only to other two which directly bear on the final proposition of this second part of it.

IV.

The first passage is the well-known description of the last judgment, which is contained in the 25th chapter of Matthew. Every child remembers it. It was read as the lesson of the day. It is so plain, and so directly to the point in its bearing on the present stage of our argument, that it hardly calls for anything but to be re-read. I am not unaware of its apparent difficulties; nor ignorant of the fact, that there are expositors who do not see in it the judgment of the church, but only the judgment of the nations and kingdoms that are outside of it. However this may be, we take *the principle* that underlies the whole of the proceedings, and we cannot but think that it is deeply significant in respect to the estimation in which loving acts are held by God, and in respect to the reward with which they are ultimately to be crowned. Men as sinners are justified by faith, but that faith must be proved and manifested by works; and those works which are specially regarded as fulfilling this end, are the works which belong to practical beneficence. "Faith works by love."

"Shew me thy faith without thy works; I will shew thee my faith by my works." Without love as its soul and life, faith is dead. The proofs of a man's living and active faith will, in the coming judgment, be seen to consist in that tender and thoughtful love, which led him to clothe the naked, and feed the hungry, and visit the neglected, and remember the forgotten. All these things Christ will recognize as done to himself, though it might be in the person of one of the least of his disciples; and then shall be fulfilled, in the most transcendent manner, his own animating prophetic assurance, "a cup of cold water, given to a disciple, in the name of a disciple, *verily I say to you, it shall in no wise lose its reward.*"

The second passage is the parable before us, from which the text of this discourse is taken, and out of which the whole of our protracted argument sprang. It is felt by many to be very difficult. One thinks its morality to be questionable, because it seems to approve the villany of the steward: and another thinks its doctrine dangerous, because it appears to encourage a sort of popish dependence upon good works. I don't think you are likely to be disturbed by either of these conceits. I have often told you to look at *the spirit* of a parable, to mark its general scope and specific lesson, and not to attempt to make every little particular significant. It was not *our* Lord you will understand who commended the steward for having done wisely. It was *his* Master or Lord who did that. Now both of them belong to the same sphere—the Lord and the steward; both are of the world, and look at all things in the low, coarse, and secular light of it. Hence, the one seeks to conciliate—by a stroke of policy, involving crime—the good-will of those who may serve him in a season of anticipated destitution. He induces them to become parties to a fraud, so that more motives than one might secure their support. The other, when he hears of it, however he may condemn the dishonesty of the act, cannot but admit its wise adaptation to the end to be attained. "The fellow," he might have said, "is without question bad and base; but he is clever and adroit, and has certainly acted with consummate skill in taking care of himself." Nothing is praised—even by him who speaks simply as a worldly man—but the wisdom of the means by which his servant sought to accomplish his purpose. 'Look,' says our Lord, ' at what these *men of the world* say and do.' They are wiser in their generation—wiser in respect to their ultimate objects —than the children of light. They think, and plan, and construct schemes, and carry them out with skill and determination. They don't let their faculties lie torpid. If they want to compass something on which their hearts are set, they select and employ an adapted instrumentality instead of leaving things to the chapter of accidents. I say unto you learn of them.

Avoid their wickedness, but imitate their wisdom. Sanctify *the principle* of the policy of which you have heard, and, *in the spiritual sphere of thought and action to which you belong,* turn the very Mammon which in their hands is base and unrighteous to noble ends and divine results. Use it for God; employ it in beneficence. Make the poor and destitute your loving debtors. They will pray for and bless you here; many of them may precede you to the regions of light —for the poor of this world are often rich in faith and heirs of the kingdom. They will go to the better land before you; they will anticipate your coming; and when you are called thither, there will mingle with the words and greeting of the Master the hymns and the hosannas of those whom you served; they will recognize their benefactor and receive and welcome you to your "everlasting habitation." * Such is a free popular exposition of the meaning of this parable. Looked at in the light of all our previous reasonings, I am not afraid that you will either misunderstand or abuse it.

It may be proper to observe, perhaps, that the phrase " that when ye fail *they may receive you* into everlasting habitations," might be rendered *impersonally ;* that is, its real sense might be thus expressed —" at death you shall *be received* into an everlasting habitation." But the peculiar form of speech employed was no doubt chosen to preserve the parallel

* 2 Peter i. 1 ; i. 5—11.

between the use to which our Lord put the parable and the actors and circumstances of the parable itself.

We have thus completed our long argument, and feel in approaching the last word as if we were parting from an old friend. More last words, however, must yet be added before we have entirely done with the subject. We shall not, therefore, attempt anything like a winding-up of the whole matter this morning. Some practical suggestions remain to be given; some counsels and cautions insisted upon; and some application of the substance of the argument to "these our times." Postponing, however, all these till we can conveniently resume the subject, we terminate the present discourse by making one more allusion to the teaching and testimony of the Divine Word. We commend to your remembrance a passage in the second Epistle of Peter, with the reading of which the argument we have been pursuing may appropriately close, especially that last link of it which has occupied us to-day. "Simon Peter, a servant and an apostle of Jesus Christ, *to them that have obtained like precious faith with us*:—Giving all diligence, add to your faith virtue; and to virtue knowledge; and to knowledge temperance; and to temperance patience; and to patience godliness; and to godliness *brotherly kind-*

ness; and to brotherly kindness *charity.* For if these things be in you, and abound, they make you that ye shall neither be barren nor unfruitful in the knowledge of our Lord Jesus Christ: but he that lacketh these things is blind, and cannot see afar off, and hath forgotten that he was purged from his old sins. Wherefore the rather, brethren, give diligence to make your calling and election sure: for if ye do these things, ye shall never fall: for *so* AN ENTRANCE SHALL BE MINISTERED UNTO YOU ABUNDANTLY *into the everlasting kingdom* of our Lord and Saviour Jesus Christ."*

* 2 Peter i. 5—11.

PART THIRD.

Stewardship

AND

Systematic Beneficence.

Get all you can;
Save all you can;
Give all you can.
JOHN WESLEY.

Sermon XIII.

1 Cor. iv. 2.

"It is required of stewards that a man be found faithful."

Luke xvi. 10—12.

"He that is faithful in that which is least is faithful also in much: and he that is unjust in the least is unjust also in much. If therefore ye have not been faithful in the unrighteous Mammon, who shall commit unto your trust the true riches? And if ye have not been faithful in that which is another man's, who shall give you that which is your own?"

I NOW wish to secure attention to some of those practical lessons, which we should carry away with us and resolve to act upon, as the result of the discussion in which we have been engaged. To give something like order to these, we purpose to keep in view the spirit and object of the two passages which have just been read as the basis of the present discourse.

I.

You are all familiar with the idea of "Stewardship" as a Scriptural designation for the obligations and responsibilities of a Christian man. The word is sometimes specially applied to ministers—to those who sustained an official function, with its recognized relations and duties in the Church—or to those who were distinguished by spiritual gifts and supernatural endowments, conferred for the benefit of the whole body. But "Stewardship" is not confined to such. It is something which attaches to every individual, and which extends to everything that belongs to him. The Apostles were "Stewards of the mysteries of God;"* a bishop was "to be blameless as the steward of God;"† Christ spake of the faithful and wise steward, "whom his Lord should place over his household;"‡ —but this class of passages by no means exhausts the Scriptural representation.

The teaching and tendency of many of our Lord's parables convey the lesson that *all* His Servants— every individual who calls Him Master and Lord—all and each are to regard themselves as *entrusted* with something; as having put into their hands a talent or a pound,—or two or five, more or less,—with the solemn injunction "occupy, till I come."§—It is then to be seen, not only what the more eminently endowed may have achieved, but what "*every* man has gained by trading."||

In consistency with this, the Apostles appealed to

* 1 Cor. iv. 1.   † 1 Titus i. 7.   ‡ Luke xv. 42.
§ Luke xix. 13. || Luke xix. 15.

the general conscience of the body of the faithful, requiring all to act "as good stewards of the manifold grace of God;"* reminding them that when the time of scrutiny and of reckoning came, *every* man, personally and individually, would " have to give " to the Lord, "an account of *himself.*"†

Now, Christian Stewardship, in its largest and most comprehensive sense, includes everything in a man's talents, education, culture, influence ;—his office in the Church, his position in the world ;—his intellect, heart, conscience, capacity ;—his family relations and personal endowments ;—whatever is in him, or about him, or within his reach, that can be employed for usefulness,—that can be cultivated and trained to perfect and beautify his own nature, so as at once to please and to glorify God,—or that can be directed to promote the benefit of others, or to advance the general good,—all and everything of which it is possible to conceive that the man may be required to give an account,—enters into the *material*, so to speak, of that of which every Christian man is to be considered a Steward. But all that we have to do with at present, is the statement that, according to the teaching of the New Testament, *Money* is *part* of this diversified and complex possession.

It cannot be necessary to do more than simply to assert this. It needs no proof. The whole of the

* 1 Peter iv. 10.　† Rom. xiv. 12.

argument through which we have gone, rests on the fact of the Stewardship of money. That there should be precepts and commands in relation to the use of it;—that obedience to these should be acceptable and remembered;—that future account, recognition, and reward, should be indicated or promised—points, you remember, which were fully proved,—all this proceeds on the assumption that money is a *trust;*—that God is to be regarded as the real owner of it;—that whatever amount of it any man possess, he is to understand that he holds it for *Him*, and holds it under certain conditions;—that as God could have withheld it at first, or given it to another, or could at any moment resume it and take it out of his hands, so He has a right to prescribe what is to be done with it, and to demand an account of it whenever he pleases, or whenever the period of Service terminates. All this our past argument has proved and illustrated almost to weariness; but no part of it can have force or significance except on the preliminary admission of the fact that money is a serious and important part of what constitute the material of Christian Stewardship.

Instead of proving, indeed, what is so obvious,—so palpable as a matter of fact, from the very constitution of things, and so absolutely necessary to be admitted as a logical basis for the entire teaching of the New Testament,—instead of anything so gratuitous, it would be more to the point, to remind you that the whole of the argument, including both parts, goes to illustrate not merely the fact that money is a trust, and that it must be dealt with on the principle of stewardship,—but that it is one of the most serious and influential of those diversified elements which go to make up the sum total of that for which men are to be called to give account. The importance of money, thus viewed, arises from the fact of its capacity to represent everything else; from its power to do harm if perverted and abused, and its power to do good, if properly employed for that purpose. The *love* of it is "the root of all evil;"— the *use* of it, as in God's sight, may express and illustrate all virtue. In the illustration of the statement that Money may be a bad thing, you saw how it might blind a man to truth; darken the intellect, harden the conscience, excite passion, corrupt the heart; keep a man out of the kingdom of God, or hinder that kingdom in getting into *him*. You saw how it provoked persecution; how it debased the Church; how it led to lying, induced hypocrisy, occasioned backsliding, tempted some into error, or even worse, so that "they taught what they ought not for filthy lucre's sake;" and how it exasperated in others "many deceitful and hurtful lusts, that drown men in destruction and perdition." You saw these things, and many more; you heard the threatenings uttered against those of the rich who lived in neglect of the obligations of their Stewardship, —that their gold "should consume them, and eat their flesh as it were fire;" that they should "utterly perish in their own corruption," and be "as wandering stars, to whom is reserved the blackness of darkness for ever!" In addition to this bad influence of money, in prompting and exasperating all evil, in the case of those who abuse and pervert it, you saw, in the other picture, (the second part of our argument,) how, when rightly regarded and religiously employed, Money might be the means of illustrating the virtues of the Christian life; developing the principles on which it rests; manifesting, and making visible, and setting in the sunlight the divine beauties which distinguish and adorn it. By money, *instrumentally*, the Christian may express faith in God, love to Christ, love to the world, brotherly kindness; sympathy, disinterestedness, largeness of heart, liberality of disposition; a grateful sense of redeeming mercy; practical consecration to the Saviour's service; the possession and culture of that "mind that was in Christ Jesus,"—imitation of His spirit in vicariously interposing on behalf of others by suffering and sacrifice. Everything that is noble, amiable, God-like; divine in its source, beneficent in action; everything that can contribute to the lightening and lessening of the load of evils which afflict humanity,—that can illustrate the genius and spirit of the Gospel,—beautify individual character, and tend to elevate the general life of the Church,—all these things, and many more, may be exhibited and embodied in the practical uses to which money may be put by a Christian man. Hence, looking at both the evil and the good, we feel warranted in saying that the point to be noticed is, not the mere fact that money must be regarded as *a part* of the material of Christian Stewardship, but that, from its representative character, its multiform influence, its capacity to become the outward and visible sign of what is inward and unseen,—spiritual or devilish,—it ought to be considered *as one of the most important and testing things with which a man or a Christian can possibly be entrusted.*

II.

The second thing to be noticed is, that we should try to get a clear and practical notion of what Stewardship implies, and should keep this in view and honestly apply it to the Stewardship of money.

Of course, what we have been saying all along takes for granted that you already understand what is meant by Stewardship. You do not need to be taught that. Nor, indeed, are we proposing to teach it, or to set it before you as a thing of which you know nothing.

Assuming your acquaintance with the matter generally, we only wish to help you a little in giving clearness to your conceptions, and depth and intensity to your convictions about it.

The general idea of the office of a steward, as presented in Scripture, is that of a house-steward; —one who is placed over a large domestic establishment; who has to keep all accounts, and to be answerable for every item of expenditure. To this indoor idea, however, there is sometimes added what more especially belongs to our notion of a bailiff;— a person who has the management of an estate,—a farm or vineyard,—sheep-station or cattle-run, as the case may be,—and who has to buy and sell,—to lay out whatever it may be necessary to expend,—to dispose of the produce, and to carry the profit to the account of the owner.* There are not wanting, within the limits of this metropolis of ours, instances of persons whose office corresponds to these definitions. In the houses of the nobility, there are those who have to regulate and superintend the establishment, and to see to its various expenditure; while, in the city, there are concerns which, though not literally farms and vineyards, are more valuable and productive than either, and over some of these there are persons placed in such positions of power and responsibility that, according to their own judgment, they

* Math. xx. 8. Luke viii. 3; xii. 42; xvi. 1.

buy and sell, receive and export,—continue or withdraw confidence in customers,—engage or dismiss subordinate servants;—thus acting on behalf of minor, absent, or sleeping principals, who entrust everything to their fidelity and confide in matters being so managed as to accrue to their advantage. That is Stewardship. It is the acting on behalf of another;—especially where property is so entrusted to any one, and is *so under his control*, that it may by him be wasted or diminished by fraud, indolence, or incapacity, or worked to a profit and made constantly and increasingly valuable. Without, however, taking either of these higher representatives of the office as the exact type of what is meant,—or deeming it necessary to find a correspondence in every particular between it and our practical Christian man,—we think it enough to say, that a steward may be regarded as one who *in any way* is the agent of another,—a servant subject to authority;—who may be in the shop, or the warehouse; the farm or the bank; in any employment, in fact, in which time and attention, faculty and skill, the brain and the hand, behove to be engaged in doing the business, promoting the interests, guarding and increasing the property of another. Every one of you, who, in any way, are thus circumstanced; who are not your own masters; who are accountable to those whom you are engaged to serve,—you can all feel the point and application of this general statement. You are all stewards,—whether clerks, warehousemen, heads of departments, travellers, agents, drapers' assistants, or anything else,—if you have to work for others; if your time is theirs; if your skill and ability are required to be exercised in their behalf; if their rules and injunctions are imperative upon you; if *they* direct, prescribe, control, and what *you* have to do is to obey. If you are entrusted with any duty or office whatsoever,—accountable for the proper discharge of its obligations, and liable to have the trust withdrawn or confirmed by those who gave it,—you are, to all intents and purposes, *stewards;* you have a Stewardship or agency, which you are bound to conduct according to the mind and with a view to the advantage of those whom you serve, "*for it is required of stewards that a man be found faithful.*"

Stewardship, then, is service, agency, acting for another. The individual so engaged, is well aware that money or goods placed in his hands are not *his*. They belong to the proprietor, and he has to deal with them as such. He cannot apply them to his own advantage. They must be disposed of according to the will and object of the master, and for his ultimate benefit. But this is not all. Stewardship dignifies and elevates the idea of service, by associating with it *trust* and *confidence:*—the employer asking for the *mind* of the servant, and not merely for his hands and feet. A slave, working like a machine,—watched by the eye of the overseer,—goaded to his labour by the lash,—is not a steward, in any allowable sense of the word; hardly more so than a horse or a bullock. Those servants who are really stewards are those in whose *honour*, so to speak, confidence is placed :—from whom is expected, not merely the perfunctory discharge of their prescribed duties, but the exercise of thought, interest, ingenuity, skill in *so* doing their allotted work as best to realize the idea of their employer. Such men feel that their time is not their own, nor their business-talents, nor any culture, experience, or knowledge they may possess which may be used to promote the success of the concern. They make the interests of their employers their own. They feel that they are looked to, at once to prevent waste and loss and any abuse by which their Principal might be injured, and so to give themselves to what they have to do, as to do it with all their mind and with all their might, that it may turn out to be effective and successful. While doing this, they have a reward —not only from the inward satisfaction of the conscience, but in an adequate payment in the form of salary;—sufficient, say, for the maintenance of that social position which may properly belong to them. This will be the case if their employers are simply just; but if they are kind, considerate, generous, there will often be the frank encouraging acknowledgment of the value of their services, their fidelity and devotion,—and, now and then, at the end of a year, or on some occasion when there is a special investigation into the condition of the concern and a review of the conduct of its agents, there may be a substantial acknowledgment of past service, in the form of a valuable gift or bonus,—or even by such a change of position as may transfer the man from the lower standing of a servant or steward to the higher level of a principal or proprietor. Having been found "faithful in that which was another's,"—the result is, that he becomes possessed of "property of his own."

III.

In the third and last place,—let us proceed to apply these common-sense views of secular stewardship to the subject before us—the Stewardship of money,—money *in the hands of a Christian man*.

A Christian is one who has given himself to Christ, and is professedly God's servant and son,—bound to act as in God's sight, to do everything according to his conceptions of "the will of God concerning him," subjecting himself and all his concerns to the law of the kingdom. His Stewardship is, primarily, *moral and spiritual*. Accepted through the exercise of repentance and faith; trusting, as a sinner, in the

Divine mercy; rejoicing in hope of reconciliation, and in the consciousness of a subjective spiritual change by the "washing of regeneration, and the renewing of the Holy Ghost,"—the work which he has to do, and which emphatically constitutes his spiritual Stewardship, is, in Scripture language, this: —he has "to perfect holiness in the fear of God;" he has "to keep his heart with all diligence;" he has to aim at progressive "sanctification;" he has "to grow up into Christ in all things;" he has to repress the motions and "crucify the lusts of the flesh;" his conduct and behaviour are in all respects to be "becoming the Gospel of Christ;" he is to endeavour always and in everything "to be pleasing to God;" he is "to exercise himself" to have "a good conscience," "a conscience void of offence towards God and man;" his reason and intellect, his passions and affections are all to be cultivated, governed, and exercised, so that he may faithfully discharge the duties of his position, "Serve his generation," and glorify God; he has to live "not to himself"—"to look, not only on his own things but also on the things of others;" he has "to increase and abound in love," not only towards "the household of faith," but "towards all men;" he has to dress and adorn his soul with those graces and ornaments of the spirit, which "in the sight of God are of great price;" he has to yield obedience to

T

the laws of Christ, and to study to be like Him; he has to be careful "not to grieve the Spirit of God;" he has "to live by faith;" on faith as a principle he has to rear the edifice of Christian character,—for he has "to add to his faith virtue, and to virtue knowledge, and to knowledge temperance, and to temperance patience, and to patience godliness, and to godliness brotherly kindness, and to brotherly kindness charity;" he has thus "to give all diligence" that "he may be perfect and entire, wanting nothing;"—so that, being "neither barren nor unfruitful," having cultivated his vineyard, and improved his talents, and kept that with which he was entrusted, he may receive at last the glad welcome, "well done, good and faithful servant; thou hast been faithful in a few things, I will make thee ruler over many things, enter thou into the joy of thy Lord."

Such is the divine and spiritual aspect of that work to which a Christian is called as "the Steward of God." His Stewardship of money is to be looked at *in its relation to this*. In the hands of one entrusted with wealth—*the principle* applies whether a man has little or much—money properly used will bear upon the culture, the advance and development of every part of this spiritual process. We can only, at present, give you the merest outline of a train of thought illustrative of the bearings of the subject before us. Keeping in mind what was formerly advanced in respect to secular business, you will easily see the point of our remarks without any formal or minute explanations.

A Christian man, being the servant and steward of God, *nothing* that he has is his own. Every thing he possesses is a trust. It belongs to Him "whose he is, and whom he serves." His money, therefore, is God's. It is committed to him as one of the instruments (and a very important one it is) by the proper and conscientious use of which, he may accomplish the moral and spiritual work given him to do. If he does not use it properly—if he is not conscientious in what he does with it—the effects on himself, his character and condition, may be most disastrous.

A man may do three things with his money. It may be *spent, saved, given;*—under *giving* you may include *lending*. There may be some so circumstanced as to be able neither to "save," nor "give;" and even for what they "spend," they may be indebted to others. But we have not to do with extreme and exceptional cases. Supposing a Christian man to have a competent income, then we say that, entrusted by God with the Stewardship of money, his *spending, saving,* and *giving* must all be regulated by conscientious principle; by the presiding and regulating thought, that for what he does with it in each case, he stands solemnly accountable to God.

It is not wrong to be rich. Riches may come by God's blessing and from Him. If they increase, He does not say throw them away,—but, " Set not your heart upon them ;" let them help you to be "rich in good works;" by your possession and use of them you may glorify me. As it is not wrong to be rich, it cannot be wrong to save. It is wise and right, a duty and an obligation, and if done conscientiously, for proper purposes, and in the fear of God, it may call forth, foster, and develope, some of the strongest elements of the Christian character. As to spending, why, money must be spent from sheer necessity; men must live and be accommodated, and must purchase what is necessary, and they must pay for it,—and a Christian must "owe no man any thing." But besides this, it is quite proper for a man to spend in proportion to his fortune, income, and rank. It is one of the duties, in fact, as we have before said, of those who *have* money, to spend it. They thus contribute to the general good, by furnishing employment and aiding those who depend on trade.

So, again, money is to be employed in acts of beneficence. It is to be *given*. The Stewardship of wealth very emphatically includes this. The wants and claims of man as man; all the forms of indigence and suffering ; the sphere of the philanthropist; the work of the Church—its mission and obligations to the ignorant at home, and the heathen abroad ; all these call for money, and every Christian entrusted with it is bound to give of it to these objects.

Now, just as a steward, servant, or agent in any secular concern has to feel that his *mind* is his master's, as well as his hands, and that his attention, thought, tact, talent, should be vigorously and faithfully given to the interests of his employer; so, we say, the Christian Stewardship of money demands, on the part of God's servant, in respect to every form of its use and disposal, the exercise of reflection; a reference to conscience; the recollection of responsibility to God; attention to the appeals of humanity as addressed to the ear of justice and love. Everything is to be weighed as in the balances of the sanctuary; a decision formed; and then energy, skill, schemes and plans wisely constructed, prudential limitations or beneficent liberality as may seem best. Spending, saving, giving, or lending, all being done so as best to meet what may be felt to be *the Master's will*, and what may best evince at once the wisdom and the fidelity of his servant.

Again : in proportion to the trust confided to a steward, much may be left to his intelligence and honour as to the manner in which he may discharge his obligations. Instead of stringent rules and specific prescriptions regulating his procedure, the nature and end of his office may be defined, but in carrying it out he may have to be "a law unto himself." Now, this is precisely the case as to the Christian Stewardship of money. God has given no precepts definitely regulating *expenditure*. He has not said how much or how little is to be *saved*. He has not required that any specific per centage on property or income, is imperatively to be laid aside to be *given away*. Nor, with the exception of the poor in general, and poor relatives in particular, and some forms of religious offering, has He indicated any objects to which gifts are to be devoted.* Everything is left to principle and conscience, to judgment and wisdom, faith and love. It is for the man himself to decide how much he will give,—and to what he will give it,—and in what manner. Whether he gives much or little; gives it publicly or privately; to persons or societies; in legacies or subscriptions;— builds a church, supports a missionary, establishes an hospital, founds almshouses, endows a college, lends to an individual, or gives a park to the public,—all is to be determined by the man himself. He must exercise his judgment, consult experience, calculate consequences, make his election, and refer *himself* and his *doings* to the judgment of God and the revelations of eternity. The great thing is obedience to conscience, —loyalty to duty,—solicitude to be in harmony with the divine will; " for it is required of stewards that a man be found faithful."

* Gal. ii. 10. Rom xv. 26, 27. 1 Tim. v. 4. Gal. vi. 6.

Once more: conscientiousness in relation to the Stewardship of money, will, in a devout man, promote conscientiousness in respect to the higher spiritual duties of the divine life. "He that is faithful in that which is least," may be expected to be faithful "in that which is much." That is to say, he that wisely and religiously uses the instrumentality of mammon, will be most likely to be diligent and devoted in the discharge of the duties of spiritual religion and the general culture of the inner life. The habit of fidelity in the lower sphere, will at once be promoted by fidelity in the higher, and will re-act on the furtherance of that. No man can be really conscientious, *on religious grounds*, in any one department of duty, without other departments being influenced and stimulated by it for the better.

Finally: the Master whom the Christian serves, is not merely just but infinitely generous. The conditions of stewardship are not the terms of bargain and hire, but of promise and grace. God's servants, while they live and work, have a maintenance secured to them,—at the very lowest they have "food and raiment,"—their "bread is given and their water is sure." But very often they have far more than that. Corn and wine, and pleasant fruits, and robes, and jewels, and goodly estates,—the abundance of the earth and the fulness of the sea; and along with these, all the blessings that enrich the heart,—the visits of the loving Father of spirits—the sunlight of His love—the consolations of the Comforter; the calm tranquillity of a good conscience and a contented mind; "the peace which passeth all understanding." They have good wages while doing their work; an adequate income,—and that not so much the hire of a servant, as the allowance of a son. But in the end, —when their account is given in, their services recognized, and their fidelity acknowledged,—then will it be seen that, having been "faithful in the use of the unrighteous mammon," they shall be for ever endowed with "the true riches"—the spiritual riches of the upper world. Having been *faithful* "in that which was *another's*,"—that which they *held in trust for God*, and which all along they knew to be *His*,— God Himself shall give to them "that which shall be their own." The glory with which they shall be invested, and the possessions which shall be theirs, will be something which shall enter into the very essence of their being; shall become a part of themselves; shall not be a means or instrument but *an end;* and shall not be subject therefore to any of the uses, conditions, and restraints of that probationary service to which everything entrusted to us belongs here.

Sermon XIV.

1 Cor. xvi. 2.

"Upon the first day of the week let every one of you lay by him in store, as God hath prospered him, that there be no gatherings when I come."

OUR attention was directed last Sunday morning to an illustration of Christian Stewardship, with special application to the Stewardship of money. We saw that money was not only *one* of the things of which a Christian man is constituted a steward, but one of the most important;—the *love* of it constituting the root of all evil,—the conscientious use of it being adapted to foster, develope, and manifest all virtue. We investigated and explained the position of a steward in relation to secular matters, especially dwelling on the point that he was one in whom confidence was placed, and who, in the mode of fulfilling his obligations, had a good deal left to his wisdom and discretion. We saw, too, how, in common life, the sagacity, diligence, and conscientious fidelity with which such services and duties are discharged, were often followed by acknowledgment and recompense, though the prospect of that was not presented as the motive of action—the source of the conduct acknowledged and rewarded. In conclusion, we briefly adverted to the analogy that might be observed between secular and Christian Stewardship in their obligations and issues, from the nature of the case, and the gracious constitution of things under the Gospel.

To-day, according to the intimation of last Sunday, we propose, for the most part, to confine our attention to what has been called "systematic beneficence,"— that is, to the mode, or one of the modes, in which the Stewardship of Money may be most efficiently carried out.

I.

The matter is very plainly and very fully put—at least the *principle* of it is distinctly embodied—in the words of the text. "On the first day of the week let every one of you lay by him in store, as God has prospered him." On this Paley wrote—now getting on to near a hundred years ago,—"by which I understand St. Paul to recommend what is the very thing wanting with most men, *the being charitable upon a plan;* that is, upon a deliberate comparison of our fortunes with the reasonable expenses and expectation of our families; to compute what we have to spare; —and to lay by so much for charitable purposes in some mode or other." Hence, you see, though the phrase " systematic beneficence " is of very modern use,—and the Society that advocates it is one of the newest of our institutions,—the idea it embodies was caught and exhibited by Paley long before the most of your societies existed; and *he* found it in the writings of the Apostle, standing out with a distinctness and clearness which could not be overlooked; and it had stood there, before the eye of the church, from the first years of the Christian era.

Let us then look at this rule or recommendation of St. Paul;—ascertain its import;—and illustrate its advantages.

The full and proper sense of the text is this:—

" *On the first day of the week,*"—that is, of every week;—"*let every one of you lay by him in store,*"—that is, each one, privately, at home, setting something apart and treasuring it up;—let him do this " *as God has prospered him,*"—that is, in proportion to his income from whatsoever sources that may arise, or according to the amount of wealth which God in His providence may at any time allot to him.

Such is the recommendation. The reason assigned for it is founded on its expediency—" *That there be no gatherings when I come,*"—that is to say, " that on my arrival, instead of having to call you together, and to re-state the object of the collection, and to press it upon you, and to stimulate your zeal, and to evoke your liberality, and to gather up what you might then be influenced to give, all shall be ready beforehand;—ready and given, not as the result of urgency on my part or of constraint and necessity on yours, but as a matter of deliberate preparation, and individual voluntary assessment;—nothing will have to be done, but for each to pay in when the opportunity is offered the amount of his conscientious, weekly storing, whatever it may be."

II.

On all this we remark,

In the first place:—That we have no wish to claim for this recommendation of the apostle, the character of a distinct and authoritative divine law, as if it were something like one of the commands of the decalogue. It comes to us, not so much as the utterance of the regal will of the Head of the Church, as the wise suggestion of the experience and sagacity of one of his servants. *The thing to be done* was indeed imperative. It was the law of Christ that Christians should "bear one another's burdens;" that "if one member suffered, others were to suffer with it;" that those who "had this world's goods," were "to communicate" and to "distribute," and to "minister" to the wants of the necessitous, especially to their brethren of "the household of faith." *This* was matter of positive obligation. It could not be neglected by those concerned without sin. But *the mode* of carrying it out, or of preparing for doing so, was a matter simply of wisdom and expediency, to be adopted or not according as it approved itself to a man's own judgment;—provided, always, that he fully and fairly examined the suggestion, thought of it and weighed it with candour and impartiality, and looked at it in the light of a living conscience as well as in that of the mere understanding. After doing so, if even one of the disciples at Corinth had *not* laid by in store *every week*, but, when the apostle came, had contributed to the collection *his adequate proportion as regulated by the amount of his property and income on a review of the whole of the time to which the apostle's advice applied*, it is not to be supposed that he would have been thought guilty of a sin for having done in one way what Paul had recommended to be done in another, seeing that the thing itself which was to be done, actually *was* done. At the same time, he might have lost something,—some benefit or advantage to himself, while following his own course instead of that suggested by the apostle; and the apostle, without blaming him as if guilty of sin, might yet think, that his adoption of his advice, and especially his being *known* to *adopt* rather than to *reject* it, would have contributed, in many ways, to the benefit of the brethren and the interests of the Church.

In proof, however, of what we have advanced, you may observe that the recommendation in the text was a special suggestion referring to a particular thing; to something that was then to be accomplished, and which, being accomplished, was to be, so far, and for the time, *done with*. The weekly storing, so far as the special object was concerned, would then cease. The apostle was raising, throughout Galatia, Macedonia, and Achaia, a collection for the Christian poor of Jerusalem. He wished to obtain as much as possible;—and, as the time during which the money was to be contributed extended over a good many months, more indeed than a year, he advised or directed the members of the different Churches to lay aside something every week, as God prospered them, that when the time came for his sending or taking their benevolence to Judea, the amount might not only be ready, but have been steadily accumulating all the time, week by week.

It is obvious, from the circumstances of the case, that when the money was collected, and the apostle had received it, and he and his associates had taken it away, the business was accomplished, and the whole thing finished—so far as that particular contribution was concerned. The advice of the apostle had been followed; it had produced its fruit; and the season for which it was given had closed. The people had to lay by in store, for a special object, every week, *till* he came to receive their liberality. After he was gone, they were not required to go on storing for that *special object*—but they might, if they pleased, continue the practice for *other* objects. Whether they would do so, might depend, not only on the wisdom and excellence of the plan itself, but on their own zeal, conscientiousness and devotion; their apprehension of the claims of Christian Stewardship; their application to its duties of intelligence and skill; and their purpose " to make full proof " of their fidelity.

You may further notice, that, in addition to the special and temporary object to which the apostle's advice applied, there were the usual claims on the Corinthian Christians to be met, for which the weekly storing, *here recommended*, was not available. We know, not only from the nature of the case, but from many intimations in the New Testament, that money had to be raised in the first Churches for many purposes. The ministry had to be supported, —" for they that preached the Gospel were to live of the Gospel:"—the indigent poor, especially widows and orphans, had to be provided for;—expenses would be incurred for places to meet in, and for what was needed for the decent administration of the Lord's Supper every first day,—besides other requirements that might be mentioned. But for all these, the apostle's advice in the words before us *did not apply.* For these, the money put away was not available. He wanted a specific contribution for a specific purpose;—to obtain this, he recommended a private, weekly laying by of a certain sum by every man; but this was altogether distinct from the ordinary calls and claims of the Church, the ministry and the poor, which all had to continue to contribute to as before;—the special storing being additional to all this, a temporary, pressing call for a distant community. In like manner, then, as we said before, when the matter was accomplished the apostle's advice had done its work, and so far, and in relátion to that, ceased and determined as a matter of course. The Churches were then free from attending to that special, supplementary contribution in relation to which the advice was given, and had only to attend to the ordinary claims upon them,—the demands of which had never been remitted. How far they might continue to act on the apostle's advice, and so meet *these* by applying it to *them*, we do not know. That would depend, as we have already intimated, on their wisdom or their piety. It would not be sin if they ceased to practise weekly storing when the work was done for which it had been recommended. But they might be very unwise for not continuing it. They might lose much by giving up a mode of action of which their recent experience might have taught them the advantage. That, however, they had to decide for themselves. It was one of those things which was left to the judgment and discretion of the steward, which he might adopt or not, so long as, honestly and conscientiously, and to the utmost of his power, he pursued the ends and objects of his Stewardship. The *principle* involved in the apostle's recommendation, is applicable to all time. All that we say is, that the advice as to a specific mode of procedure, being, from the then existing circumstances, specially applicable to a particular case, we cannot and do not claim for it the urgent character of a positive and authoritative divine law.* It may have in it, nevertheless, a ray of that wisdom "which cometh from above, and which is profitable to direct," and be itself a practical, regulative maxim "to which we shall do well if we take heed."

III.

Observe then, in the next place, that though we do not place this rule of procedure on a level with the authoritative " shalts " and " shalt nots " of the ten commandments; though we do not say that it is to be regarded as, in such a sense, "a law of Christ," and so binding on the conscience, as not to be disregarded without sin;—yet we do say, that there is in it such profound sagacity, that it is so admirably adapted to meet the circumstances and to provide for the

* 2 Cor. viii. 8—10.

accomplishment of the work of the Church, that the Corinthians would have been wise if they had continued to act upon it when the temporary necessity was past for which it was given;—and that we of the present day would do well to return to it, to adopt it and carry it out, if we would so discharge our Christian Stewardship as at once to do fully and perfectly what God requires of us, and to do it with comfort and satisfaction to ourselves.

Observe briefly the following things:

1st. We have nothing to do at present with proving the duty, or enforcing the obligation, of giving money to religious and benevolent objects,—devoting it, say, to God, by devoting it to works of usefulness or mercy, in obedience to His will and under the influence of religious faith. All that is taken for granted. We assume that you admit it. The apostle assumed it in the passage before us:—he says nothing about the obligation of the Corinthians to contribute, only about the mode in which the duty might be discharged. He had taught them their duty many a time, just as, in the course of our previous argument, we are willing to hope that we have convinced you of yours. Assuming this to be acquiesced in and felt by the Corinthians, the one thing before the mind of St. Paul, and the one thing that now comes before us, *is the best way of carrying out what on all hands is admitted must be done,—*

namely, the *giving of money* so as "*to serve our generation according to the will of God.*"

2nd. This being understood, then we say, in the words of Paley, that, what the Apostle recommended "is the very thing wanting with most men, the *being charitable upon a plan.*" That is, as he proceeds to explain, "upon a deliberate comparison of our fortunes with the reasonable expenses and expectations of our families; to compute what we have to spare; and to lay by so much for charitable purposes, in some mode or other." These words, you will observe, include the three things—"spending," "saving," and "giving"—which we comprehended in the Stewardship of money when describing it last Sunday,—which, as was said, were all to be regulated by principle and conscience. They are all involved in St. Paul's recommendation of "systematic beneficence," and are each glanced at in the quotation just read from the eminent author already named. "Being charitable" or beneficent "*on a plan;*"— that is, "on a deliberate comparison of our fortunes" —annual income, business profits, weekly wages, as the case may be—"with the reasonable expenses and expectations of our families." "Expenses and expectations," —that is, *spending* and *saving*. Both are to be "reasonable,"—that is, the style of "expenditure" must be wise and consistent, suitable to position and means; the "expectations" of children must be limited to what is moderate and just; *both* the expenses and expectations—spending and saving—must be calculated in connexion with another item for which allowance must always be made, namely, an amount *to be given away*. Hence, the next thing, " the *deliberate comparison* " of our fortunes or income with what may " reasonably" or justifiably be spent, or saved—is to be connected with a " computation," founded upon it, of "what can be spared ;" and then *this* is to be " laid by," to be disposed of in such modes and for such objects as may approve themselves to the judgment and conscience. All this is involved in the language of St. Paul. And it amounts, as has been said, and will bear to be repeated, to that which is just the thing "wanting in most men,"—charity *on a plan;* in other words, " systematic beneficence."

3rd. Notice, in the next place, that "the deliberate comparison," the " computation," the calm determination of "what can be spared to be laid by for charitable purposes," all this, which in any thoughtful and virtuous man of the world, would be the exercise of prolonged thought, prudence, wisdom, and benevolence, —all this, is not only to be found in a Christian man, and found as the result of the same exercises of intellect and feeling, but they are to be connected with such sacred associations, and such holy duties, as shall elevate them into what is spiritual and divine.

The collection, referred to by St. Paul, was for "the saints"—*God's* "saints;" his recommendation was, —"on the first day of the week,—let every one,—apart by himself,—lay aside, as God has prospered him." Notice how the idea of God runs through the whole texture of the advice. How thoroughly the men are addressed as having to act as in God's sight, and as entrusted by *Him* with the Stewardship of their money; and how emphatically Christian ideas, and Christian exercises of mind and heart, are to mingle with all their calculations and purposes. The object for which they were to store was sacred;—it was for *the saints;* for those in whom, as they had been taught, the Master himself was to be seen; that Master who had died for them, and who had said that, if required, they in like manner should be ready "to lay down their lives for the brethren." They were to separate and set apart what was to be given to God, *on the first day of the week;*—that is, in connexion with those hallowed recollections which were connected with that day,—Christ risen from the grave, "the resurrection and the life," after having died on the cross "to take away sin;" the day sacred to the breaking of bread, and early song, and associated service—when the heart of the church was more than usually alive and awake to the greatness of God's "unspeakable gift." They were to regulate the amount of what was to be devoted, "*as God had prospered them,*"—literally, as matters had prospered or gone well with them; but, as all things were felt by Christian men to be in God's hands, and that every measure of prosperity was from Him, the Divine name is properly introduced here by our translators. It was intended that there should be present the penetrating thought that everything was held as a gift from God; that all came from Him and came as a trust; and that, in giving to Him a Christian could only give Him back His own. And lastly, every man was to make his personal appropriation *privately* and at home,—that is the force of the apostle's expression. There is a great deal involved in this. The man was to be alone, but alone with God. He was to be removed from the influence of numbers and publicity, which might be dangerous to the simplicity and purity of his motives. He was to do what he did as a religious act,—as in God's sight—in connexion, of course, with prayer for the help and guidance of His Spirit, and with protracted thought adapted at once to remind him of his obligations and to quicken his conscience to acknowledge and enforce them. All this, you observe, is fairly suggested by the words of the text. Hence, we say, that this setting apart of a certain portion of our income to God, is not only a thing which requires thought, calculation, comparison of resources and expenditure,—but that all this, in a Christian man, must be attended to in connexion with the exercise of faith and prayer,—with the realization of the Divine presence,—the recollection of the facts of the redemption, so adapted to stimulate love to Christ,—and the repression of everything from within and without, that might in any way interfere with the action of the conscience, or hide from the man what the master would seem to have him to do as "a good steward of the manifold grace of God."

4th. In the fourth place, you will next observe that, while the rule of action here laid down by St. Paul assumes that beneficence is felt to be a duty; while it prescribes a mode of procedure which requires serious thought, accuracy and exactness in pecuniary accounts, that a man may know precisely how he stands and what he is worth,—elaborate calculation of all sorts of claims upon him, present and prospective, that his spending, saving, and giving, may all be fairly and equitably adjusted,—while it involves all this,—and *so* puts the matter, that this looking into accounts, and settling expenses (cutting them down, or extending and enlarging them,) with every other mental exercise, shall be most solemnly and most emphatically *religious*,—a thing conducted under the influence of sacred associations, with the eye of the conscience fixed on the transaction, the man realizing the presence of God—seeking His aid, and contemplating His glory;—while all this, and far more than this, is implied in the text, you will observe that he says nothing as to *how much* any one is to give, or by what scale they are to regulate the sum they set apart for God. The matter is left to the individual himself. The appeal is made to every man's conscience. As to the amount that every one appropriates, he must be " a law unto himself." The apostle prescribes nothing. He does not ask for a tenth, or for a fifth, or any other specified portion. He makes no assessments. He leaves that to the voluntary decision of the Christian himself,—presupposing him to be actuated by spiritual views, free by the law of liberty but constrained by the law of love. The only prescription is, that *giving to God* shall be PROPORTIONATE to *receiving from Him*. Every man is to give *as* God has prospered him :—that is, according to his income, from whatever it may arise. But how much of that he is to set aside,—twenty pounds in a hundred, ten, or five,—all that is left to the individual conscience. Each man may lay down a law for himself, but no man is to *enforce* a law upon another.

IV.

It is commonly supposed that among the Jews, under the Mosaic law, the people had to give *a tenth* of their annual income to religious objects; that this was imposed upon them by statute, nothing being left to the judgment or will of the individual. And it has been thought, that the amount of *God's* assessment laid on the ancient church *by law*, should be that which, under the Gospel, a Christian should lay *upon himself* by *love*. It will be worth a little time to look into this matter, and worth a few words, if we can succeed in enunciating a fair and accurate conclusion respecting it.

The following things should be noticed. 1st. In the laws of Moses you find *two* tenths, or tithes, expected from the people, out of every year's income. The first tithe was a strictly Mosaic impost,—a thing originating in the Desert, springing out of the political and ecclesiastical arrangements then and there made or provided for. It went exclusively to the tribe of Levi, in its two unequal divisions into Priests and Levites. The whole of the tithes,—the tenths paid by the entire people,—were given to the Levites, and then the Levites gave each a tenth of his portion of these to the priests.*

But there was a second tithe. The tenth of all the increase of the field, vineyards, flocks, herds, etc., was to be appropriated to God and to the poor,—the man himself coming in for his own share of it.†
This second tithe was to be employed in offerings at the temple, and in social, sacrificial feasts, of which the man and his family partook, and to which he

* Numb. xviii. 26. † Deut. xiv. 23.

was required to invite the poor, the stranger, the Levite, the widow and the fatherless, that they might all rejoice before the Lord, in the acknowledgment of his hand and the enjoyment of his gifts. This tithe does not seem to have originated with Moses. He does not enforce it as a new thing. It is rather taken for granted as an existing custom, and is only *regulated* by some new enactments. It is supposed to have been the continuance of that tithe, or tenth, which Jacob at Bethel vowed to devote to God.* If he acted on his vow, (and we must suppose that he did,) nothing is more probable than that his descendants continued the custom after him; and as neither he nor they, previous to the giving of the law, had any separated *caste* to support, the further probability is, that it was "given to God" (in the language of Jacob) by being employed in beneficent acts,—in helping and cheering the poor,—and in contributing to such inexpensive religious observances as at that time prevailed.

It may here be noticed, that some have thought that what we have just described as a second tithe was really a second *and third*, and that there were *two* tenths taken, one for religious offerings, and one for social and charitable feasts. We prefer, however, considering that both these came out of one tithe. In after times, when the people determined to have a

* Gen. xxviii. 22.

king, Samuel told them that he would take from them a tenth of all their income to support his State and to give to his servants.* If that ever was the case, then, for political, ecclesiastical, and charitable purposes, the Jewish people were taxed to the extent certainly of *three* tenths of their income,—some say four; but three tenths, 30 per cent., is in all conscience a sufficiently serious amount.

Leaving out, however, the last two tithes we have mentioned, we limit attention to the other two—each of which is distinctly provided for in the enactments of the Mosaic law,—and we say, that, instead of a *tenth* of their income being expected of the Hebrews for ecclesiastical and other objects, what they had to give was really two tenths, or a fifth.

2nd. In the second place, it should be noticed, that though these two tithes were to be furnished by the people,—the one a new impost and prescribed by the law, the other recognized by the law as an understood thing, and expected as the continuance of a custom;—yet in both cases, obedience was very much left to the individual conscience. Even the first tithe that was expressly required for the support of the Levitical order, does not seem to have been recoverable by any legal process, if any one neglected or refused to tender it. It was left to every man's principle and honour; and yet it is to be observed,

* 1 Sam. viii. 15.

that this tithe can hardly be regarded as a *benevolence*. It was given to the tribe of Levi in lieu of that landed property which would have been theirs if the country had been divided into twelve parts instead of eleven. Levi had no inheritance.—Each of the tribes had in consequence so much more than they otherwise would have had; they had each one-eleventh more than their share; and they had to give a tenth of their produce for that,—which, considering that it was not only instead of it, but *as payment for all the duties* which the Levitical tribe undertook, not only in the temple-service, but in various other ways, I don't know that the amount was at all disproportioned or inequitable. At any rate, it is evident, that this consideration materially alters the character of the tithe. It appears more like *a payment* than a benevolence, and yet even for *this* there does not seem to have been any positive *exaction*. It was left to the individual conscience to prompt compliance and enforce payment.

The second tithe was more emphatically a benevolence. It was an offering to God and the poor; it was not given *in lieu* of anything, but was an assessment on what a man had "according as God had prospered him," and was devoted to religious and charitable objects. But this, too, though recognized and regulated by the law, was still left to be rendered according to the individual conscience. There was no process or provision for enforcing it. There was however a solemn form of words prescribed to be used, which would secure the benefaction from every man who had a conscience and who dared to use the form. A man might be negligent in rendering his benevolence one year,—and even a second; but every third year he was expected to square accounts,—to render, in full, everything that he owed to God and the poor, and then to stand at the altar and make a solemn declaration that he had done so. *Thou shalt say before the Lord thy God,*—"I have brought away the hallowed things out of mine house, and also have given them unto the Levite, and unto the stranger, and unto the fatherless, and to the widow, according to all thy commandments which thou hast commanded me: I have not transgressed thy commandments, neither have I forgotten them: I have not eaten thereof in my mourning, neither have I taken away ought thereof for any unclean use, nor given ought thereof for the dead: but I have hearkened to the voice of the Lord my God, and have done according to all that thou hast commanded me. Look down from thy holy habitation, from heaven, and bless thy people Israel, and the land which thou hast given us, as thou swarest unto our fathers, a land that floweth with milk and honey." In this way was obedience secured. The extent or the amount of the gift was prescribed, but the actual rendering of it was suspended on the movements of the conscience, and on a religious transaction between the man and God.

3rd. But it may be observed, in the next place, that, in addition to the two tithes mentioned, the Jewish people had to give the firstlings of the flock and the herd; had to redeem by money or destroy the firstborn of unclean animals that could not be sacrificed; to redeem their own firstborn, and to make other ecclesiastical payments, besides the *first fruits* of the field and vineyard; so that *even if we put aside the first tithe as being a real charge,* and limit their religious and benevolent contributions to the second,—the firstlings, the first fruits, redemption money, freewill offerings, and special benefactions,— the amount that the members of the ancient church were expected and required to give was far more than a tenth of their annual produce. *Therefore*, no law can be deduced from what *they* did, which shall *limit* the members of the Christian Church to a tenth of their income in laying up or setting aside a portion of it for God.

4th. It would thus seem, that no precise and definite rule, in respect to what a man is to give, can be drawn from the Old Testament. A tenth, at least, cannot be determinately fixed; for *that would not be enough*,—it would not be equal to the standard to which (by hypothesis) the man would think that he conformed. As to the New Testament, it is understood and admitted that it prescribes nothing but the duty,—the importance of religious and benevolent contribution. The amount to be given, the scale of assessment which a man applies to his property or income, the objects to which he devotes what he lays aside, the mode in which he separates, or stores it, or gathers it together, the way in which he disposes of it, as to time or circumstance;—all this is left to the conscience of the individual, as God's servant, entrusted by Him with the Stewardship of money, and as accountable to Him for whatever he does with it.

V.

From the whole of this discourse we may gather at least the following things:—

1. That Christian men, especially men of property, or of fair and competent income for their position in life, ought not to leave the amount of what they give to religious and charitable objects, to be determined by circumstances; by appeals from without; by the impulse of feeling; by congregational excitement, and such like. If they do, they may give capriciously and unwisely. They will be liable to be irritated by solicitations. They will be sure to fancy that they are " always giving," and that they give a great deal more than they really do,—the probability being that

they most likely give a great deal less than they ought.

As to being worried by incessant applications, it may be well to remember, that this species of "persecution" is perhaps the form of trial which belongs to an advanced state of the world and the Church; and that it is one which some who have lived before us would have thought very light compared with their own. In a distant age, when the Church was in the ascendant, and society consisted only of the wealthy and the poor, the Few built and endowed churches for the benefit of the Many, founded monasteries, schools, or halls of learning having thus to express their piety towards God. Afterwards when the middle class rose into importance, and religious reformations, free thought, and individual enquiry gave birth to so-called heresies and schisms, the resolutely conscientious had to be prepared for martyrdom, to stand in the pillory, lose their ears, be branded on the cheek, rot in prison, fly the country, suffer the spoiling of all they possessed! They had not our thousand and one Societies to support, with collectors coming round as a perpetual annoyance. But *their* trial was something far worse,—something which we of the present day would hardly choose instead of our own. Now that all classes are more upon a level, and wealth is diffused on all hands,— when the battle has been fought and the victory gained,

—our fathers having suffered that we might enter on what was purchased by their tears and blood,—society is in that condition which brings demands to the Many as well as the Few, and the Church is exposed to no persecution worse than a constant appeal to the pocket! To the rich, then, and to all, it may well be said,—Be thankful. You have not been called to bleed like your fathers. Accept the trial (if you feel it to be one) of your own times; bear it with cheerfulness, and rejoice in God that it is so light.

2nd. That, to obviate complaint, and to secure fidelity in the discharge of God's stewardship, Christians ought to regulate their beneficence *by a plan;* they ought to be as systematic in appropriating what they intend to give, as, if they are wise, just, and economical, they are in regulating their saving and expenditure. This, however, will require thought and calculation, serious and deliberate, prosecuted in connexion with all such spiritual recollections and exercises, as shall make the whole of what they do and determine the result of religious faith. If they do this, they will be saved from many annoyances. They will find giving will become easy and pleasant. They will never feel worried, or put out of temper, by an appeal for something. They will not get irritated, and answer abruptly, and refuse rudely, and then be angry with themselves from the consciousness of having done wrong,—a consciousness that stung them at the time, and was one of the causes of their bad temper. They will be saved from all that, for they will have either something to give on all occasions, or a good, conscientious reason why they have not. Instead of waiting till objects are presented, and people find them out, they will often be able and inclined to go in search of them. By acting upon a plan, many a humble Christian with limited means, will be ready to give largely, when richer men, who leave everything to chance, will either give less, or give nothing at all,—on the plea that they really cannot afford it!

3rd. As to the New Testament rule of giving, there is no law, but simply the general principle that, while it is to be *proportionate*—every one giving less or more "as God hath prospered him,"—the extent or limit of the voluntary assessment is left for each to determine, according to his own knowledge of his circumstances, and to the promptings of faith, wisdom, and love. The whole thing is put under the control of religious feeling and moral principle. The way in which St. Paul puts it is—" every man, according as he purposeth in his heart, so let him give; not grudgingly, or of necessity, for God loveth a cheerful giver." "If there be first a willing mind, it is accepted according to that a man hath, and not according to that he hath not." "But," he adds, "this I say, he that soweth sparingly, shall reap also sparingly, and he that soweth bountifully shall reap also bountifully."* To a loving, conscientious, Christian man the rule of giving will be, not so much what he can *spare*, what can be afforded after supplying superfluities,—but how much God has a *right to*,—how much would seem to be equitably required. In fixing upon this, which it is left to himself to determine, he will be influenced by the thought, that the Lord who died for him, and appeals only to his gratitude and affection, may be supposed to address him in words like these,—" I might *enjoin* thee that which is convenient, yet for love's sake, I rather *beseech;*" "Albeit I do not say to thee, how *thou owest* unto me *even thine own self besides.*"†

4th. If any one lays down for himself the rule of devoting a tenth of his income to God, he does well. If all Christians would do that, there would be enough and to spare for all the objects of Christian beneficence. There would be no need for rates or imposts, taxes or endowments of any sort whatever. Ministerial support—the building and repairing of churches and schools—the expenses of worship—congregational societies—Home, Colonial, and Foreign missions—with every other form of philanthropic activity, all would be provided for by a tenth being taken from the sum total of the income of the Church.

* 2 Cor. ix. 7; viii. 12; ix. 6. † Philemon 8, 9, and 19.

It is to be remembered, however, that for some, a tenth of their income would be too much, while for others it would be far too little. A man with a wife and ten children, or a less number than that, in the position of a clerk, with a hundred or a hundred and fifty pounds a year, is not to be told that he is subject to a law requiring him to give away, in spite of the multiplied claims of his household, a tenth of his narrow and limited resources; nor is a rich Christian, with fifty thousand a year, to be told that he does any very great thing, or that he discharges the obligations of his divine stewardship, if he gives *five* thousand per annum away, and keeps *five and forty thousand* to himself. A *tenth* is a fair proportion, as things are, for the great mass of the middle classes, with average incomes tolerably competent to their position; but it is not an amount which can be equitably applied to extreme cases on one side or the other;—the struggling and necessitous,—the opulent millionaire,—the very poor, or the very rich.

Such are some of the conclusions to which we are brought, by that particular subject of discourse which has occupied us to-day. There are many things that might yet be included in this series of sermons on money,—on the use and abuse, the perils and advantages of wealth. I am afraid, however, of wearing out your patience, and of deadening attention, by the monotony of so prolonged and protracted an argument as the one we have been pursuing. I shall now, therefore, wind up the whole matter by two or three concluding remarks.

VI.

1st. In respect to giving, you will understand that our Lord's words, enforcing the doing of alms "in secret," are not of universal application. What he forbade was the wrong motive,—the doing a thing *with the view* to be seen of men. He condemned ostentation, not simply publicity. He himself saw what the poor widow did, and he approved it. She could not help so giving her mite that the action could be seen, but she did not do it *to be seen*, not even by Christ. Christ himself did many kind and loving acts—alms of the noblest sort—openly, before all; but he did not in this transgress his own law. The fact is, there are important ends to be observed by your "light being made to shine before men;"* by many of your contributions being public,—with your names appended and declared. Just as Paul says, in respect to the Corinthians, "your zeal hath provoked very many;"† and as John says respecting Gaius, and says with approval, that "many had borne witness to his charity before the church."‡ There is

* Math. v. 16. † 2 Cor. ix. 2. ‡ John iv. 6.

such a thing as the force of example, and "the provoking of others to love and to good works."*

2nd. But it is very important, so far as we ourselves are concerned, "not to let our left hand know what our right hand doeth;"—that is, not to talk to *ourselves* of what we do; not to think of it, and be elated by it. The great thing in this matter is simplicity and *unconsciousness*. *God* will not forget what we do; but we ought. It should be enough for us that our gifts are remembered in heaven. Christ even represents the righteous, at the last day, as being unconscious of having done any great thing. They did not know what they had done till reminded and told of it—told of it by *Him*.

3rd. Hence, thirdly, though we are quite sure that beneficent acts will be followed by reward, we are not to do them *with a view to that*. It cannot be wrong sometimes to remember what God has promised, and to be influenced in a degree by His own encouraging declarations based on the reality of the future recompense. But the great thing is, to love Christ,—and so earnestly and gratefully to be devoted to his service, that we "do good and communicate" because we cannot help it. The instincts and impulses of the Divine life make it a necessity. We find a sufficient reward in the work itself, without anxiously

* Heb. x. 24.

calculating on any other. As to expecting anything from men, I have long learnt the profound wisdom of our Lord's rule—" do good, give alms, hoping for nothing again." Yes; do good, and go on doing it, *hoping for nothing again*, not even thanks. If they come, well. If not, never mind;—go on and do more good; *you* don't need the thanks, but others, even the thankless, may very much need your donation.

4th. Though every man is to be a law to himself in this matter, and though it is not for us to judge any one, yet it is of no use for rich Christians to shut their eyes to the fact that their conduct will be observed, and that, if they are never known to do anything at all proportioned to their means, the inference will be, that what they ought to do is not done. It is not for them to pretend to despise this; or to take refuge in Christ's words enjoining secrecy; or to stand on the ground of their being accountable to God and not to man; or that they do what they think right, and nobody else has any business with it. The fact is, people *have* business with it. A rich Christian has a duty towards the Church,— towards the faith which he professes, and the Master he serves,—a duty requiring the shining of the light, the influence of the example, of which we have already spoken. A Christian reputation has to be maintained,—and God's people have to be encouraged,—by the large and copious liberality of the rich. It is looked for,—and people have a right to look for it. Close-fistedness in a man known to have ample means, discourages others; affords an excuse to many who want one, for withholding what *they* ought to give; and provokes at once the grief of the good,—the sneer, contempt, or laughter of the profane.

VII.

As a practical conclusion to the particular topic handled to-day, I commend to you, not only the habit of being benevolent on a plan, laying aside a fixed sum according to your ability, and as the result of thought and prayer,—but I commend to you the support of THE WEEKLY OFFERING recently commenced in this place. I do not regard this as the exact fulfilling of the apostle's advice, but only as a partial and limited result of it. The apostle's recommendation is to be obeyed in private;—in the weighing of circumstances, and fixing upon an amount, and laying it aside, literally or in intention; then, this being settled, the weekly offering will come in for a *part* only of what most of you are able to devote to God.

It is quite legitimate for the weekly offering to go to one or two things only,—just as we saw that what

Paul recommended at Corinth was to go to a specific object, while all ordinary claims continued to be met in some other way. So, our weekly offering is to meet all the expenses required to carry on the worship of God in this place, all that we term "incidental;" and, in addition to that, we wish it to amount to such a sum as will thoroughly supplement the donations and subscriptions to the Congregational Societies, — keeping them always efficiently at work, and free from debt. If it should do more than this, we shall be glad and thankful; but if it does this, we shall be satisfied. The way to make it succeed, is *for every individual, every Sunday, to put in something, however small the amount.* Don't forget the offering. Don't neglect it. Don't think you can put in more one day if you pass it by on another. You MAY,—but you may *not*. If you fall into such a habit, you will fail altogether. Cultivate the other habit,—the habit of *always* giving something. It will get fixed. It will prove pleasant. It will become a necessity. The thing will be a success. You will contribute to and secure that; and, depend upon it, you will find your account in it, and " be blessed in your deed."

May the blessed God, whose holy will we have been endeavouring to ascertain and to set forth, in this long discussion, graciously grant His blessing to our work! May He impress on the reason the arguments we have used in support of the truth, —and carry to the conscience, and write upon the heart, the practical lessons we have sought to set forth. May He mercifully pardon infirmity and error; and so far give witness to his own word, that the fruit of these discourses may appear in the conduct of many of you now, and be crowned hereafter with the approving welcome of the Great Master, by whom "*it is required of his stewards*—THAT A MAN BE FOUND FAITHFUL." Amen.

*** I cannot dismiss this last sheet without referring to the invaluable services of the Rev. John Ross, who for several years has devoted himself to the inculcation of the duty of "weekly storing" for God. He has laid many churches under lasting obligations to him by discovering to them the secret of their undeveloped and unsuspected strength; and he has been the means of greatly increasing the happiness and usefulness of many rich men, through their being led to act in accordance with his lessons. I fear my worthy friend will hardly be satisfied with the way I have treated his proof-text—the text of this last discourse. I have put it, however, as it shaped itself to me when engaged upon it; and it is at least doubtful whether a fresh investigation would alter my impressions.

ILLUSTRATIVE NOTE

To page 308. "For some a tenth of their income would be too much, while for others it would be far too little. A man with a wife and ten children, or a less number than that, (say seven) in the position of a clerk (or a clergyman) with a hundred or a hundred and fifty pounds a-year, is not to be told that he is to give away a tenth of his narrow and limited resources."

As I am closing my labours on this book, and sending away the last proof, I find in the "Times" of this morning (November 16th) a letter of "An East-end Incumbent," from which I take the following extracts :—

"Much sympathy has been expressed of late by all classes towards those who labour earnestly to obtain an honourable living; but there is one class of workers whose case appears to be somewhat overlooked. I allude to the curates of poor and populous parishes in the destitute portions of the Metropolis.

"The Ecclesiastical Commissioners are doing all in their power to raise the incomes of incumbents to £300 a-year, but nothing has been done by any society or commission to augment the stereotyped £100 per annum which is usually offered to a parochial curate. No one, therefore, need wonder why it is that the supply of educated gentlemen to fill such positions is rapidly diminishing. It is simply impossible for a gentleman to live in London on such an inadequate stipend. Lodgings are more expensive, the wear and tear of clothing is greater, the calls of poverty upon the purse are more numerous, and the opportunity of enjoying the hospitality of their parishioners is far less frequent than with their brother curates in country parishes, and it is really high time that some effort should be made to increase the salary of every curate working hard in a large and poor parish to at least £150 a-year.

* * * * *

"There are in the three deaneries of St. Sepulchre, which includes Shoreditch, Spitalfields, and Stepney, 73 curacies; of these about 13 are now vacant; and I have no hesitation in saying that they will continue vacant unless some of the societies *or some wealthy and charitable Churchmen come forward liberally* and help to augment the stipends offered. Few of them are more than

£100 per annum, a sum altogether inadequate for the support of a clergyman even if unmarried, much more so if he be in the position of *a curate now labouring in one of the poorest districts* of the East-end, *who has a wife and seven young children, and only £100 a year to support them with.* It is stated on authority that this clergyman, who dispenses the bread of life faithfully to others, *has often not enough of earthly bread to feed his children with.*

* * * * *

"There is a vast amount of wealth in London, and a vast amount of poverty. *The one must help the other.* It would be a sad spectacle for us to see the east arrayed against the west— the poverty-stricken against those who enjoy every luxury; and it cannot be denied that the over-worked and underpaid curates of the east, who do all they can to mitigate the miseries of the destitute, are, even in a financial point of view, well worth the £150 with which they would be content.

"In behalf of the poor committed to their charge, rather than their own, I venture to ask the powerful aid of the ' Times ' in placing this grave and important subject *before the wealthier classes of the Metropolis.*"

If this book comes into the hands of any rich Churchmen, I trust its arguments and appeals may, by God's blessing, have some effect in evoking their liberality in behalf of such cases as those referred to. How can a man, with a wife and seven children to support, and the position and appearance of a gentleman to maintain on a hundred a-year, have his mind free from distraction so as to give its energies to the composition of sermons or to anything requiring intellectual effort? Even an unmarried curate, on his £100 or £150, will find it difficult to get books to keep himself abreast of the critical and theological utterances of the times. In the absence of better provision, and with the feeling that a gift of money might be unwelcome, *a present of first-rate books* might be made without impropriety, and would be highly valued by many who need but have not the means to procure them. May these words bear fruit, not only among Churchmen, but among the rich of other denominations, to whom they may be equally suggestive and equally applicable!

www.ingramcontent.com/pod-product-compliance
Lightning Source LLC
Chambersburg PA
CBHW030736230426
43667CB00007B/737